GROWING IN PATIENCE AND PURPOSE

GROWING IN PATIENCE AND PURPOSE

A Special Edition of *Waiting on God* and *Working for God*

First Edition: Year 2023
Growing in Patience and Purpose / Outreach, Inc.
Paperback ISBN: 978-1-958585-32-0
eBook ISBN: 978-1-958585-33-7

CHURCHLEADERS
PRESS

Colorado Springs

GROWING IN PATIENCE AND PURPOSE

A Special Edition of

WAITING ON GOD *and* WORKING FOR GOD

ANDREW MURRAY

ENDURING FAITH FOUNDATIONS

CHRISTIAN LIVING

CHURCHLEADERS
PRESS

Colorado Springs

CONTENTS

WORKING FOR GOD

INTRODUCTION
to the *Enduring Faith Foundations Series*

*B*ooks in the *Enduring Faith Foundations Series* cover a multitude of discipleship topics including non-fiction works on effective prayer, fruitful Christian living and more, and include important literary fiction as well—great books that have enthralled and challenged people for generations. In this series you will find works by best-selling authors like Andrew Murray, a South African writer, teacher, and pastor; F. M. Bounds, an American author, attorney, and prominent Methodist; and Charles Sheldon, pastor of a Congregational Church in Topeka, Kansas, and best known for challenging millions with the question: "What would Jesus do?"

Whether you are new to the books and authors in this series, or are turning to them again as so many have over the years for their wisdom and encouragement, here are some of the features you will find in the SPECIAL EDITION versions of the books in this series that help make these fresh and accessible for a new generation of readers:

- While diligent to faithfully preserve the original voice and style of the central text of each book, the addition of **light annotations** easily found next to the referenced text as **side notes in the margin** make these books accessible and understandable. This feature is especially helpful for younger readers who may be less familiar with some of the more obscure references.

- Remember, you aren't meant to tread the walk of faith alone! Each
  volume in the series includes a suggested **reading plan and discussion
  questions**. "As iron sharpens iron" (Proverbs 27:17a), you are
  encouraged to read them with others. Whether reading in concert
  with a friend, parent/child, mentor/mentee, or in conjunction with a
  small group or book club, to get the most out of these books, read and
  discuss together with at least one other person.

In addition to the features noted above, enjoy the **comfortably wide margins** to jot down your own notes or doodles. You'll also find **space to write** under the discussion questions included in the back of the book.

I hope that along with spending time in the Bible and in personal prayer, you are also in discipleship with others and that these books help to encourage you and grow your faith in Christ.

—Matthew Lockhart,
Project Manager

A WORD ABOUT ANDREW MURRAY AND *WAITING ON GOD* AND *WORKING FOR GOD*

*A*ndrew Murray (1828-1917) was born in Cape Town, South Africa, and became a leader in promoting missionary outreaches throughout South Africa. He served pastorates in Bloemfontein, Worcester, Cape Town, and Wellington, but is best remembered for his devotional writings. During sixty years of ministry in the Dutch Reformed Church of South Africa, he authored more than 200 books and tracts. He was also active in promoting social reform and founding educational institutions such as the Bible and Prayer Union and the Huguenot Seminary, where young women could prepare for educational work.

Andrew Murray wrote at a time when devotional books were flooding bookstores. And, as you'll discover, his style is reminiscent of countless other authors who wanted to prompt readers to praise God.

But Murray wasn't content to stop there...and that's why his books remain relevant and read more than a hundred years after his death.

Unlike many of his contemporaries, Murray drilled deeply into foundational issues that Christians then—and now—sometimes find uncomfortable.

In *Waiting on God*, Murray challenges believers not to dash off to do good without waiting for clear direction—and strength—from God. Though Murray was passionate about encouraging missions and supporting practical reforms to improve the lot of his parishioners in South Africa, he still cautioned his readers to wait.

To wait for God's guidance. And God's power. And God's timing.

In *Working for God*, written by Murray as a sequel to *Waiting on God*, he tackles the practicalities of serving God and serving people in God's name. Yes, there's a call to evangelism and service, but unless believers have a sincere desire to allow God to work in and through them, no efforts will be truly effective.

In two months of daily devotions, Murray gently and wisely invites readers to grow closer to the God who patiently waits for us to turn to Him, and who desires to fuel our lives with his love.

So get ready for two months that may change everything.

—Mikal Keefer,
Special Edition features writer

WAITING ON GOD

Andrew Murray

PREFACE

*P*REVIOUS to my leaving for England last year, I had been much impressed by the thought of how, in all our religion, personal and public, we need more of God. I had felt that we needed to train our people in their worship more to wait on God, and to make the cultivation of a deeper sense of His presence, of more direct contact with Him, of entire dependence on Him, a definite aim of our ministry. At a "welcome" breakfast in Exeter Hall,[1] I gave very simple expression to this thought in connection with all our religious work. I have already said elsewhere that I was surprised at the response the sentiment met with. I saw that God's Spirit had been working the same desire in many hearts.

The experiences of the past year, both personal and public, have greatly deepened the conviction. It is as if I myself am only beginning to see the deepest truth concerning God, and our relation to Him, centered in this waiting on God, and how very little, in our life and work, we have been surrounded by its spirit. The following pages are the outcome of my conviction, and of the desire to direct the attention of all God's people to the one great remedy for all our needs. More than half the pieces were written on board ship; I fear they bear the marks of being somewhat crude and hasty. I have felt, in looking them over, as if I could wish to write them over again. But this I cannot now do. And so I send them out with the prayer

1 **Exeter Hall:** Between 1831-1907, Exeter Hall in London was a public meeting place capable of seating 1,600 people.

that He who loves to use the feeble[2] [3] may give His blessing with them.

I do not know if it will be possible for me to put into a few words what are the chief things we need to learn. In a note at the close of the book on Law I have mentioned some. But what I want to say here is this: The great lack of our religion is, we do not know God. The answer to every complaint of feebleness and failure, the message to every congregation or convention seeking instruction on holiness, ought to be simply, What is the matter: Have you not God? If you really believe in God, He will put all right. God is willing and able by His Holy Spirit. Cease from expecting the least good from yourself, or the least help from anything there is in man, and just yield yourself unreservedly to God to work in you: He will do all for you.

How simple this looks! And yet this is the gospel we so little know. I feel ashamed as I send forth these very defective meditations; I can only cast them on the love of my brethren, and of our God. May He use them to draw us all to Himself, to learn in practice and experience the blessed art of Waiting only upon God. Would God that we might get some right conception of what the influence would be of a life given, not in thought, or imagination, or effort, but in the power of the Holy Spirit, wholly to waiting upon God.

With my greeting in Christ to all God's saints it has been my privilege to meet, and no less to those I have not met, I subscribe myself, your brother and servant,

—Andrew Murray
Wellington, 3rd March 1896

2   **Feeble:** Weak or wobbly, lacking in physical strength or stability.

3   "He who loves to use the feeble": A reference to Paul's reassuring words in 1 Corinthians 1:27.

WAITING ON GOD:
THE GOD OF OUR SALVATION

My soul waiteth only upon God [marg: is silent unto God]; from Him cometh my salvation.

PSALM 62:1 (R.V.)[4]

4   Murray's translation of choice tends to lean to the King James Version, though verses marked R.V. indicate the Revised Version, which was published in full in 1885.

5   **Manifestation:** A visible and/or public demonstration.

6   **Grace:** In this context, a God-given virtue.

*I*F salvation indeed comes from God, and is entirely His work, just as our creation was, it follows, as a matter of course, that our first and highest duty is to wait on Him to do that work as it pleases Him. Waiting becomes then the only way to the experience of a full salvation, the only way, truly, to know God as the God of our salvation. All the difficulties that are brought forward as keeping us back from full salvation, have their cause in this one thing: the defective knowledge and practice of waiting upon God. All that the Church and its members need for the manifestation[5] of the mighty power of God in the world, is the return to our true place, the place that belongs to us, both in creation and redemption, the place of absolute and unceasing dependence upon God. Let us strive to see what the elements are that make up this most blessed and needful waiting upon God: it may help us to discover the reasons why this grace[6] is so little cultivated, and to feel how infinitely desirable it is that the Church, that we ourselves, should at any price learn its blessed secret.

The deep need for this waiting on God lies equally in the nature of man and the nature of God. God, as Creator, formed man, to be a vessel in which He could show forth His power and goodness. Man was not to have in himself a fountain of life, or strength, or happiness: the ever living and only living One was each moment to be the Communicator to him of all that he needed. Man's glory and blessedness was not to be independent, or dependent upon himself, but dependent on a God of such infinite riches and love. Man was to have the joy of receiving every moment out of the fulness of God. This was his blessedness as an unfallen creature.

When he fell[7] from God, he was still more absolutely dependent on Him. There was not the slightest hope of his recovery out of his state of death, but in God, His power and mercy. It is God alone who began the work of redemption;[8] it is God alone who continues and carries it on each moment in each individual believer. Even in the regenerate man[9] there is no power of goodness in himself: he has and can have nothing that he does not each moment receive; and waiting on God is just as indispensable, and must be just as continuous and unbroken, as the breathing that maintains his natural life.

It is, then, because Christians do not know in their relation to God of their own absolute poverty and helplessness, that they have no sense of the need of absolute and unceasing dependence, or of the unspeakable

7   "When he fell...": A reference to Mankind's fall in the Garden of Eden.

8   **Redemption:** The deliverance of mankind from sin.

9   **Regenerate man:** A person who has made a radical change in terms of his relationship with God.

blessedness of continual waiting on God. But when once a believer begins to see it, and consent to it, that he by the Holy Spirit must each moment receive what God each moment works, waiting on God becomes his brightest hope and joy. As he appreciates how God, as God, as Infinite Love, delights to impart His own nature to His child as fully as He can, how God is not weary of each moment keeping charge of his life and strength, he wonders that he ever thought otherwise of God than as a God to be waited on all the day. God unceasingly giving and working; His child unceasingly waiting and receiving: this is the blessed life.

"Truly my soul waiteth upon God; from Him cometh my salvation."[10] First we wait on God for salvation. Then we learn that salvation is only to bring us to God, and teach us to wait on Him. Then we find what is better still, that waiting on God is itself the highest salvation. It is the ascribing to Him the glory of being All; it is the experiencing that He is All to us. May God teach us the blessedness of waiting on Him.

"My soul, wait thou only upon God!"[11]

10   "Truly my soul...": Psalm 62:1.

11   "My soul, wait...": Psalm 62:5.

WAITING ON GOD:
THE KEYNOTE[12] OF LIFE

12 **Keynote:** A central theme or principle.

I have waited for Thy salvation, O Lord!

GENESIS 49:18

*I*T is not easy to say exactly in what sense Jacob used these words, in the midst of his prophecies in regard to the future of his sons. But they do certainly indicate that both for himself and for them his expectation was from God alone. It was God's salvation he waited for; a salvation which God had promised and which God Himself alone could work out. He knew himself and his sons to be under God's charge. Jehovah the Everlasting God would show in them what His saving power is and does. The words point forward to that wonderful history of redemption which is not yet finished, and to the glorious future in eternity. They suggest to us how there is no salvation but God's salvation, and how waiting on God for that, whether for our personal experience, or in wider circles, is our first duty, our true blessedness.

Let us think of ourselves, and the inconceivably glorious salvation God has wrought[13] for us in Christ, and is now purposing to work out and to perfect in us by

13 **Wrought:** Made, created for.

His Spirit. Let us meditate until we somewhat realize that every participation of this great salvation, from moment to moment, must be the work of God Himself. God cannot part with His grace, or goodness, or strength, as an external thing that He gives us, as He gives the raindrops from heaven. No; He can only give it, and we can only enjoy it, as He works it Himself directly and unceasingly. And the only reason that He does not work it more effectively and continuously is, that we do not let Him. We hinder Him either by our indifference or by our self-effort, so that He cannot do what He would. What He asks of us, in the way of surrender, and obedience, and desire, and trust, is all comprised in this one word: waiting on Him, waiting for His salvation. It combines the deep sense of our entire helplessness of ourselves to work what is divinely good, and the perfect confidence that our God will work it all in His divine power.

Again, I say, let us meditate on the divine glory of the salvation God purposes working out in us, until we know the truth it implies. Our heart is the scene of a divine operation more wonderful than Creation. We can do as little towards the work as towards creating the world, except as God works in us to will and to do. God only asks of us to yield, to consent, to wait upon Him, and He will do it all. Let us meditate and be still, until we see how appropriate and right and blessed it is that God alone do all, and our soul will of itself sink down in deep humility to say: "I have waited for Thy salvation, O Lord." And the deep blessed background of all our praying and working will be: "Truly my soul waiteth upon God."[14]

14   Psalm 62:1.

The application of the truth to wider circles, to those we labor among or intercede for, to the Church of Christ around us, or throughout the world, is not difficult. There can be no good but what God works; to wait upon God, and have the heart filled with faith in His working, and in that faith to pray for His mighty power to come down, is our only wisdom. Oh for the eyes of our heart to be opened to see God working in ourselves and in others, and to see how blessed it is to worship and just to wait for His salvation!

Our private and public prayer are our chief expression of our relation to God: it is in them chiefly that our waiting upon God must be exercised.[15] If our waiting begin by quieting the activities of nature, and being still before God; if it bows and seeks to see God in His universal and almighty operation, alone able and always ready to work all good; if it yields itself to Him in the assurance that He is working and will work in us; if it maintains the place of humility and stillness and surrender, until God's Spirit has quickened[16] the faith that He will perfect His work: it will indeed become the strength and the joy of the soul. Life will become one deep blessed cry: "I have waited for Thy salvation, O Lord."

"My soul, wait thou only upon God!"

15 **Exercised:** In this context, to be put into action.

16 **Quickened:** Stimulated.

WAITNG ON GOD:
THE TRUE PLACE
OF THE CREATURE

These wait all upon Thee;
That Thou mayest give them
their meat in due season.
That Thou givest unto them, they gather;
Thou openest Thine hand, they are
satisfied with good.

PSALM 104:27, 28 (R.V.)

*T*HIS Psalm, in praise of the Creator, has been speaking of the birds and the beasts of the forest; of the young lions, and man going forth to his work; of the great sea, wherein are things creeping innumerable, both small and great beasts. And it sums up the whole relation of all creation to its Creator, and its continuous and universal dependence upon Him in the one word: "These all wait upon Thee!" Just as much as it was God's work to create, it is His work to maintain. As little as the creature could create itself, is it left to provide for itself. The whole creation is ruled by the one unalterable law of—waiting upon God!

The word is the simple expression of that for the sake of which alone the creature was brought into existence, the very groundwork of its constitution. The one object for which God gave life to creatures was that in them He might prove and show forth His wisdom, power, and goodness, in His being each moment their life and happiness, and pouring forth unto them, according to their capacity, the riches of his goodness and power. And just as this is the very place and nature of God, to be unceasingly the supplier of every want in the creature, so the very place and nature of the creature is nothing but this—to wait upon God and receive from Him what He alone can give, what He delights to give. (See note on Law, The Power of the Spirit.)

If we are in this little book at all to appreciate what waiting on God is to be to the believer, to practice it and to experience its blessedness, it is of consequence that we begin at the very beginning, and see the deep reasonableness of the call that comes to us. We shall understand how the duty is no arbitrary[17] command. We shall see how it is not only rendered necessary by our sin and helplessness. It is simply and truly our restoration to our original destiny and our highest nobility, to our true place and glory as creatures blessedly dependent on the All-Glorious God.

17 **Arbitrary:** Whimsical or given little thought.

If once our eyes are opened to this precious truth, all Nature will become a preacher, reminding us of the relationship which, founded in creation, is now taken up in grace. As we read this Psalm, and learn to look upon all life in Nature as continually maintained by God Himself, waiting on God will be seen to be the very necessity of our being. As we think of the young lions and the ravens

18   "Wait thou only...": Psalm 62:5. Also Murray's primary theme in this book and the verse he includes at the close of each daily reading.

19   Ere: Before.

crying to Him, of the birds and the fish and every insect waiting on Him, until He give them their meat in due season, we shall see that it is the very nature and glory of God that He is a God who is to be waited on. Every thought of what Nature is, and what God is, will give new force to the call: "Wait thou only upon God."[18]

"These all wait upon Thee, that thou may give." It is God who gives all: let this faith enter deeply into our hearts. Ere[19] yet we fully understand all that is implied in our waiting upon God, and ere we ever have been able to cultivate the habit, let the truth enter our souls: waiting on God, unceasing and entire dependence upon Him, is, in heaven and earth, the one only true religion, the one unalterable and all-comprehensive expression for the true relationship to the ever-blessed One in whom we live.

Let us resolve at once that it shall be the one characteristic of our life and worship, a continual, humble, trustful waiting upon God. We may rest assured that He who made us for Himself, that He might give Himself to us and in us, that He will never disappoint us. In waiting on Him we shall find rest and joy and strength, and the supply of every need.

"My soul, wait thou only upon God!"

WAITING ON GOD:
FOR SUPPLIES

The Lord upholdeth all that fall,
And raiseth up all those that be bowed down.
The eyes of all wait upon Thee;
And Thou givest them their meat in due season.
PSALM 145:14, 15

*P*SALM 104 is a Psalm of Creation, and the words, "These all wait upon Thee," were used with reference to the animal creation. Here we have a Psalm of the Kingdom, and "The eyes of all wait upon Thee" appears especially to point to the needs of God's saints, of all that fall and them that be bowed down. What the universe and the animal creation does unconsciously, God's people are to do intelligently and voluntarily. Man is to be the interpreter of Nature. He is to prove that there is nothing more noble or more blessed in the exercise of our free will than to use it in waiting upon God.

If an army has been sent out to march into an enemy's country, and tidings are received that it is not advancing, the question is at once asked, what may be the cause of delay. The answer will very often be: "Waiting for supplies." All the stores of provisions or clothing or ammunition have not arrived; without these it dare not proceed. It is no otherwise in the Christian life: day by day, at every step, we need our supplies from above. And there is nothing so needful as to cultivate that spirit of dependence on God and of confidence in Him, which refuses to go on without the needed supply of grace and strength.

If the question be asked, whether this be anything different from what we do when we pray, the answer is, that there may be much praying with but very little waiting on God. In praying we are often occupied with ourselves, with our own needs, and our own efforts in the presentation of them. In waiting upon God, the first thought is of the God upon whom we wait. We enter His presence, and feel we need just to be quiet, so that He, as God, can overshadow us with Himself. God longs to reveal Himself, to fill us with Himself. Waiting on God gives Him time in His own way and divine power to come to us.

It is especially at the time of prayer that we ought to set ourselves to cultivate this spirit.

Before you pray, bow quietly before God, just to remember and realize who He is, how near He is, how certainly He can and will help. Just be still before Him, and allow His Holy Spirit to waken and stir up in your soul the childlike disposition[20] of absolute dependence and confident expectation. Wait upon God as a Living Being, as the Living God, who notices you, and is just longing to fill you with His salvation. Wait on God until you know you have met Him; prayer will then become so different.

20 **Disposition:** In this context, the heart, mind, and character of the person praying.

And when you are praying, let there be intervals of silence, reverent stillness of soul, in which you yield yourself to God, in case He may have aught[21] He wishes to teach you or to work in you. Waiting on Him will become the most blessed part of prayer, and the blessing thus obtained will be doubly precious as the fruit of such fellowship with the Holy One. God has so ordained it, in harmony with His holy nature, and with ours, that waiting on Him should be the honor we give Him. Let us bring Him the service gladly and truthfully; He will reward it abundantly.

"The eyes of all wait upon Thee, and Thou givest them their meat in due season." Dear soul, God provides in Nature for the creatures He has made: how much more will He provide in Grace for those He has redeemed. Learn to say of every want, and every failure, and every lack of needful grace: I have waited too little upon God, or He would have given me in due season all I needed. And say then too—

"My soul, wait thou only upon God!"

21   **Aught:** Something or anything.

WAITING ON GOD:
FOR INSTRUCTION

Shew me thy ways, O Lord;
Teach me Thy paths.
Teach me Thy paths.
Lead me in Thy truth, and teach me;
For Thou art the God of my salvation;
On Thee do I wait all the day.

PSALM 25:4, 5

"*I* SPOKE of an army, on the point of entering an enemy's territories, answering the question as to the cause of delay: "Waiting for supplies." The answer might also have been: "Waiting for instructions," or, "Waiting for orders." If the last despatch had not been received, with the final orders of the commander-in-chief, the army dared not move. Even so in the Christian life: as deep as the need of waiting for supplies, is that of waiting for instructions."

See how beautifully this comes out in Ps. 25. The writer knew and loved God's law exceedingly, and meditated in that law day and night. But he knew that this was not enough. He knew that for the right spiritual apprehension of the truth, and for the right personal application of it to his own peculiar circumstances, he needed a direct divine teaching.

The psalm has at all times been a very favourite one, because of its reiterated expression of the felt need of the Divine teaching, and of the childlike confidence that that teaching would be given. Study the psalm until your heart is filled with the two thoughts—the absolute need, the absolute certainty of divine guidance. And notice, then, how entirely it is in this connection that he speaks, "On Thee do I wait all the day." Waiting for guidance, waiting for instruction, all the day, is a very blessed part of waiting upon God.

The Father in heaven is so interested in His child, and so longs to have his life at every step in His will and His love, that He is willing to keep his guidance entirely in His own hand. He knows so well that we are unable to do what is really holy and heavenly, except as He works it in us, that He means His very demands to become promises of what He will do, in watching over and leading us all the day. Not only in special difficulties and times of perplexity,[22] but in the common course of everyday life, we may count upon Him to teach us His way, and show us His path.

22 **Perplexity:** Bewilderment.

And what is needed in us to receive this guidance? One thing: waiting for instructions, waiting on God. "On Thee do I wait all the day." We want in our times of prayer to give clear expression to our sense of need, and our faith in His help. We want definitely to become conscious of our ignorance as to what God's way may be, and the need of the Divine light shining within us, if our way is to be as of the sun, shining more and more unto the perfect day. And we want to wait quietly before God in prayer, until the deep, restful assurance fills us: It will be given—"the meek will He guide in the way."[23]

23   "The meek will...": A reference to Psalm 25:9 (AM's paraphrase of).

"On Thee do I wait all the day." The special surrender to the Divine guidance in our seasons of prayer must cultivate, and be followed up by, the habitual looking upwards "all the day." As simple as it is, to one who has eyes, to walk all the day in the light of the sun, so simple and delightful can it become to a soul practiced in waiting on God, to walk all the day in the enjoyment of God's light and leading. What is needed to help us to such a life is just one thing: the real knowledge and faith of God as the one only source of wisdom and goodness, as ever ready, and longing much to be to us all that we can possibly require—yes! this is the one thing we need. If we but saw our God in His love, if we but believed that He waits to be gracious, that He waits to be our life and to work all in us,—how this waiting on God would become our highest joy, the natural and spontaneous response of our hearts to His great love and glory!

"My soul, wait thou only upon God!"

WAITING ON GOD:
FOR ALL SAINTS

Let none that wait on Thee be ashamed.

PSALM 25:3

*L*ET us now, in our meditation of today, each one forget himself, to think of the great company of God's saints throughout the world, who are all with us waiting on Him. And let us all join in the fervent prayer for each other, "Let none that wait on Thee be ashamed."

Just think for a moment of the multitude of waiting ones who need that prayer; how many there are, sick and weary and solitary, to whom it is as if their prayers are not answered, and who sometimes begin to fear that their hope will be put to shame. And then, how many servants of God, ministers or missionaries, teachers or workers, of various name, whose hopes in their work have been disappointed, and whose longing for power and blessing remains unsatisfied. And then, too, how many, who have heard of a life of rest and perfect peace, of abiding light and fellowship, of strength and victory, and who cannot find the path. With all these, it is nothing but that they have not yet learned the secret of full waiting upon God.

They just need, what we all need, the living assurance that waiting on God can never be in vain. Let us remember all who are in danger of fainting or being weary, and all unite in the cry, "Let none that wait on Thee be ashamed"!

If this intercession for all who wait on God becomes part of our waiting on Him for ourselves, we shall help to bear each other's burdens, and so fulfil the law of Christ.[24]

There will be introduced into our waiting on God that element of unselfishness and love, which is the path to the highest blessing, and the fullest communion with God. Love to the brethren and love to God are inseparably linked. In God, the love to His Son and to us are one: "That the love wherewith Thou hast loved Me, may be in them."[25] In Christ, the love of the Father to Him, and His love to us, are one: "As the Father loved me, so have I loved you."[26] In us, He asks that His love to us shall be ours to the brethren: "As I have loved you, that ye love one another."[27] All the love of God, and of Christ, are inseparably linked with love to the brethren. And how can we, day by day, prove and cultivate this love otherwise than by daily praying for each other? Christ did not seek to enjoy the Father's love for Himself; He passed it all on to us. All true seeking of God and His love for ourselves, will be inseparably linked with the thought and the love of our brethren in prayer for them.

"Let none that wait on Thee be ashamed." Twice in the psalm David speaks of his waiting on God for himself; here he thinks of all who wait on Him. Let this page take the message to all God's tried and weary ones, that there are more praying for them than they know. Let it stir

24   Galatians 6:2: "Bear ye one another's burdens, and so fulfill the law of Christ."

25   "That the love...": John 17:26.

26   "As the Father loved me...:" John 15:9.

27   "As I have loved you...": John 13:34.

them and us in our waiting to make a point of at times forgetting ourselves, and to enlarge our hearts, and say to the Father, "These all wait upon Thee, and Thou givest them their meat in due season." Let it inspire us all with new courage—for who is there who is not at times ready to faint and be weary? "Let none that wait on Thee be ashamed" is a promise in a prayer, "They that wait on Thee shall not be ashamed"! From many and many a witness the cry comes to everyone who needs the help, brother, sister, tried one, "Wait on the Lord; be of good courage, and He shall strengthen your heart; wait, I say, on the Lord. Be of good courage, and He shall strengthen your heart, all ye that wait on the Lord."[28]

28 "Wait on the Lord...": Psalm 27:14.

Blessed Father! we humbly beseech Thee, Let none that wait on Thee be ashamed; no, not one. Some are weary, and the time of waiting appears long. And some are feeble, and scarcely know how to wait. And some are so entangled in the effort of their prayers and their work, they think that they can find no time to wait continually. Father! teach us all how to wait. Teach us to think of each other, and pray for each other. Teach us to think of Thee, the God of all waiting ones. Father! let none that wait on Thee be ashamed. For Jesus' sake. Amen.

"My soul, wait thou only upon God!"

WAITING ON GOD:
A PLEA IN PRAYER

Let integrity and uprightness preserve me;
for I wait on Thee.

PSALM 25:21

*F*OR the third time in this psalm we have the word wait. As before in ver. 5, "On Thee do I wait all the day," so here, too, the believing supplicant[29] appeals to God to remember that he is waiting on Him, looking for an answer. It is a great thing for a soul not only to wait upon God, but to be filled with such a consciousness that its whole spirit and position is that of a waiting one, that it can, in childlike confidence, say, Lord! Thou knowest, I wait on Thee. It will prove a mighty plea in prayer, giving ever-increasing boldness of expectation to claim the promise, "They that wait on Me shall not be ashamed"!

The prayer in connection with which the plea is put forth here is one of great importance in the spiritual life. If we draw near to God, it must be with a true heart. There must be perfect integrity, wholeheartedness, in our dealing with God. As we read in the next Psalm (26:1, 11), "Judge me, O Lord, for I have walked in my integrity," "As for

29 **Supplicant:** Someone asking something of someone who is in power or who has authority.

me, I will walk in my integrity," there must be perfect uprightness or single-heartedness before God. As it is written, "His righteousness is for the upright in heart."[30] The soul must know that it allows nothing sinful, nothing doubtful; if it is indeed to meet the Holy One, and receive His full blessing, it must be with a heart wholly and singly given up to His will. The whole spirit that animates us in the waiting must be, "Let integrity and uprightness"— Thou seest that I desire to come so to Thee, You know I am looking to Thee to work them perfectly in me;—let them "preserve me, for I wait on Thee."

And if at our first attempt truly to live the life of fully and always waiting on God, we begin to discover how much that perfect integrity is wanting, this will just be one of the blessings which the waiting was meant to work. A soul cannot seek close fellowship with God, or attain the abiding consciousness[31] of waiting on Him all the day, without a very honest and entire surrender to all His will.

"For I wait on Thee": it is not only in connection with the prayer of our text but with every prayer that this plea may be used. To use it often will be a great blessing to ourselves. Let us therefore study the words well until we know all their bearings.[32] It must be clear to us what we are waiting for. There may be very different things. It may be waiting for God in our times of prayer to take his place as God, and to work in us the sense of His holy presence and nearness. It may be some special petition, to which we are expecting an answer. It may be our whole inner life, in which we are on the lookout for God's putting forth of

30   "His righteousness is for...": Psalm 36:10.

31   **Abiding consciousness:** An ongoing, long-lasting awareness.

32   **Bearings:** The manner in which someone behaves.

His power. It may be the whole state of His Church and saints, or some part of His work, for which our eyes are ever toward Him. It is good that we sometimes count up to ourselves exactly what the things are we are waiting for, and as we say definitely of each of them, "On Thee do I wait," we shall be emboldened to claim the answer, "For on Thee do I wait."

It must also be clear to us, on Whom we are waiting. Not an idol, a God of whom we have made an image by our conceptions of what He is. No, but the living God, such as He really is in His great glory, His infinite holiness, His power, wisdom, and goodness, in His love and nearness. Itis the presence of a beloved or a dreaded master that wakens up the whole attention of the servant who waits on him. It is the presence of God, as He can in Christ by His Holy Spirit make Himself known, and keep the soul under its covering and shadow, that will awaken and strengthen the true waiting spirit. Let us be still and wait and worship until we know how near He is, and then say, "On Thee do I wait."

And then, let it be very clear, too, that we are waiting. Let that become so much our consciousness that the utterance comes spontaneously, "On Thee I do wait all the day; I wait on Thee." This will indeed imply sacrifice and separation, a soul entirely given up to God as its all, its only joy. This waiting on God has hardly yet been acknowledged as the only true Christianity. And yet, if it be true that God alone is goodness and joy and love; if it be true that our highest blessedness is in having as much of God as we can; if it be true that Christ has redeemed us wholly for God, and made a life of continual abiding in His presence possible, nothing less ought to satisfy than to be ever breathing this blessed atmosphere, "I wait on Thee."

"My soul, wait thou only upon God!"

WAITING ON GOD: STRONG AND OF GOOD COURAGE

Wait on the Lord: be strong,
And let your heart take courage:
Yea, wait thou on the Lord.

PSALM 27:14 (R.V.)

*T*HE psalmist had just said, "I had fainted, unless I had believed to see the goodness of the Lord in the land of the living."[33] If it had not been for his faith in God, his heart had fainted. But in the confident assurance in God which faith gives, he urges himself and us to remember one thing above all,—to wait upon God. "Wait on the Lord: be strong, and let your heart take courage: yea, wait on the Lord." One of the chief needs in our waiting upon God, one of the deepest secrets of its blessedness and blessing, is a quiet, confident persuasion that it is not in vain; courage to believe that God will hear and help; that we are waiting on a God who never could disappoint His people.

"Be strong and of good courage."[34] These words are frequently found in connection with some great and difficult enterprise, in prospect of the combat with the power of strong enemies, and the utter insufficiency of all human strength. Is waiting on God a work so difficult, that,

33 "I had fainted...": Psalm 27:13.

34 "Be strong...": Words spoken by the Lord to Joshua (Joshua 1:9) and by Moses to the children of Israel (Deuteronomy 31:6).

for that too, such words are needed, "Be strong, and let
your heart take courage"? Yes, indeed. The deliverance, for
which we often have to wait, is from enemies, in presence
of whom we are impotent.[35] The blessings for which we
plead are spiritual and all unseen; things impossible with
men; heavenly, supernatural, divine realities. Our souls are
so little accustomed to hold fellowship with God, the God
on whom we wait so often appears to hide Himself. We
who have to wait are often tempted to fear that we do not
wait aright, that our faith is too feeble, that our desire is not
as upright or as earnest as it should be, that our surrender is
not complete. Our heart may well faint and fail. Amid all
these causes of fear or doubt, how blessed to hear the voice
of God, "Wait on the Lord! Be strong, and let your heart
take courage! Yea, wait thou upon the Lord!" Let nothing in
heaven or earth or hell—let nothing keep you from waiting
on your God in full assurance that it cannot be in vain.

The one lesson our text teaches us is thus, that when
we set ourselves to wait on God, we ought beforehand to
resolve that it shall be with the most confident expectation
of God's meeting and blessing us. We ought to make up our
minds to this, that nothing was ever so sure, as that waiting
on God will bring us untold and unexpected blessing. We
are so accustomed to judge of God and His work in us by
what we feel, that the great probability is that when we
begin more to cultivate the waiting on Him, we shall be
discouraged, because we do not find any special blessing
from it. The message comes to us, "Above everything,
when you wait on God, do so in the spirit of abounding
hopefulness. It is God in His glory, in His power, in His
love longing to bless you that you are waiting on."

35 **Impotent:** In this usage,
unable to take action or
achieve a goal.

36   **Wretched:** Unhappy or miserable.

37   **Warrant:** Justification.

38   At the time of this writing, it was thought therapeutic to move, if possible, weak patients into hospital courtyards to soak in sunshine and fresh air.

If you say that you are afraid of deceiving yourself with vain hope, because you do not see or feel any warrant in your present state for such special expectations, my answer is, it is God, who is the warrant for your expecting great things. Oh, do learn the lesson. You are not going to wait on yourself to see what you feel and what changes come to you. You are going to WAIT ON GOD, to know first, WHAT HE IS, and then, after that, what He will do. The whole duty and blessedness of waiting on God has its root in this, that He is such a blessed Being, full, to overflowing, of goodness and power and life and joy, that we, however wretched,[36] cannot for any time come into contact with Him, without that life and power secretly, silently beginning to enter into us and blessing us. God is Love! That is the one only and all-sufficient warrant[37] of your expectation. Love seeks not its own: God's love is just His delight to impart Himself and His blessedness to His children. Come, and however feeble you feel, just wait in His presence. As a feeble, sickly invalid is brought out into the sunshine to let its warmth go through him,[38] come with all that is dark and cold in you into the sunshine of God's holy, omnipotent love, and sit and wait there, with the one thought: Here I am, in the sunshine of His love. As the sun does its work in the weak one who seeks its rays, God will do His work in you. Oh, do trust Him fully. "Wait on the Lord! Be strong, and let your heart take courage! Yea, wait on the Lord"!

"My soul, wait thou only upon God!"

WAITING ON GOD:
WITH THE HEART

Be strong, and let your heart take courage,
All ye that wait for the Lord.

PSALM 31:24. (R.V.)

*T*HE words are nearly the same as in our last meditation. But I gladly avail myself of them again to press home a much-needed lesson for all who desire to learn truly and fully what waiting on God is. The lesson is this: It is with the heart we must wait upon God. "Let your heart take courage." All our waiting depends upon the state of the heart. As a man's heart is, so is he before God. We can advance no further or deeper into the holy place of God's presence to wait on Him there, than our heart is prepared for it by the Holy Spirit. The message is, "Let your heart take courage, all you that wait on the Lord."

The truth appears so simple, that some may ask, Do not all admit this? where is the need of insisting on it so specially? Because very many Christians have no sense of the great difference between the religion of the mind and the religion of the heart, and the former is far more diligently cultivated than the latter. They know not how infinitely greater the heart is than the mind. It is in this that one of the chief causes must be sought of the feebleness of our Christian life, and it is only as this is understood that waiting on God will bring its full blessing.

Proverbs 3:5 may help to make my meaning plain. Speaking of a life in the fear and favor of God, it says, "Trust in the Lord with all your heart, and lean not upon your own understanding." In all religion we have to use these two powers. The mind has to gather knowledge from God's word, and prepare the food by which the heart with the inner life is to be nourished. But here comes in a terrible danger, of our leaning to our own understanding, and trusting in our understanding of divine things. People imagine that if they are occupied with the truth, the spiritual life will as a matter of course be strengthened. And this is by no means the case. The understanding deals with conceptions and images of divine things, but it cannot reach the real life of the soul. Hence the command, "Trust in the Lord with all your heart, and lean not upon your own understanding." It is with the heart man believes, and comes into touch with God. It is in the heart God has given His Spirit, to be there to us the presence and the power of God working in us. In all our religion it is the heart that must trust and love and worship and obey. My mind is utterly impotent in creating or maintaining the spiritual life within me: the heart must wait on God for Him to work it in me.

It is in this even as in the physical life. My reason may tell me what to eat and drink, and how the food nourishes me. But in the eating and feeding my reason can do nothing: the body has its organs for that special purpose. Just so, reason may tell me what God's word says, but it can do nothing to the feeding of the soul on the bread of life[39]—this the heart alone can do by its faith and trust in God. A man may be studying the nature and effects of food or sleep; when he wants to eat or sleep he sets aside his thoughts and study, and uses the power of eating or sleeping. And so the Christian needs ever, when he has studied or heard God's word, to cease from his thoughts, to put no trust in them, and to awaken his heart to open itself before God, and seek the living fellowship[40] with Him.

This is now the blessedness of waiting upon God, that I confess the impotence of all my thoughts and efforts, and set myself still to bow my heart before Him in holy silence, and to trust Him to renew and strengthen His own work in me. And this is just the lesson of our text, "Let your heart take courage, all you that wait on the Lord." Remember the difference between knowing with the mind and believing with the heart. Beware of the temptation of leaning upon your understanding, with its clear strong thoughts. They only help you to know what the heart must get from God: in themselves they are only images and shadows. "Let your heart take courage, all ye that wait on the Lord." Present it before Him as that wonderful part of your spiritual nature in which God reveals Himself, and by which you can know Him. Cultivate the greatest confidence that, though you cannot see into your heart, God is working there by His Holy

39   "Bread of life": A reference to Jesus' words in John 6:35.

40   Living fellowship: A dynamic personal relationship.

Spirit. Let the heart wait at times in perfect silence and quiet; in its hidden depths God will work. Be sure of this, and just wait on Him. Give your whole heart, with its secret workings, into God's hands continually. He wants the heart, and takes it, and as God dwells in it. "Be strong, and let your heart take courage, all ye that wait on the Lord."

"My soul, wait thou only upon God!"

TENTH DAY

WAITING FOR GOD:
IN HUMBLE FEAR AND HOPE

Behold, the eye of the Lord is
upon them that fear Him,
Upon them that hope in His mercy;
To deliver their soul from death,
And to keep them alive in famine.
Our soul hath waited for the Lord;
He is our help and our shield.
For our heart shall rejoice in Him,
Because we have trusted in His holy name.
Let thy mercy, O Lord, be upon us,
According as we wait for thee.

PSALM 33:18-22 (R.V.)

*G*OD'S eye is upon His people: their eye is upon Him. In waiting upon God, our eye, looking up to Him, meets His looking down upon us. This is the blessedness of waiting upon God, that it takes our eyes and thoughts away from ourselves, even our needs and desires, and occupies us with our God. We worship Him in His glory and love, with His all-seeing eye watching over us, that He may supply our every need. Let us consider this wonderful meeting between God and His people, and mark well[41] what we are taught here of those on whom God's eye rests, and of Him on whom our eye rests.

41   **Mark well:** Take note of.

42 **Condescension:** An attitude or reality of superiority.

43 "Who shall not fear Thee...": Revelation 15:4.

44 "Praise our God...": Revelation 19:5.

45 "To fear the glorious...": Deuteronomy 28:58.

46 **Self-abasement:** A humbling of oneself.

"The eye of the Lord is on them that fear Him, on them that hope in His mercy." Fear and hope are generally thought to be in conflict with each other; in the presence and worship of God they are found side by side in perfect and beautiful harmony. And this because in God Himself all apparent contradictions are reconciled. Righteousness and peace, judgment and mercy, holiness and love, infinite power and infinite gentleness, a majesty that is exalted above all heaven, and a condescension[42] that bows very low, meet and kiss each other. There is indeed a fear that has torment, that is cast out entirely by perfect love. But there is a fear that is found in the very heavens. In the song of Moses and the Lamb they sing, "Who shall not fear Thee, O Lord, and glorify Thy name?"[43] And out of the very throne the voice came, "Praise our God, all His servants, and ye that fear Him."[44] Let us in our waiting ever seek "to fear the glorious and fearful name, The Lord thy God."[45] The deeper we bow before His holiness in holy fear and adoring awe, in deep reverence and humble self-abasement,[46] even as the angels veil their faces before the throne, the more will His holiness rest upon us, and the soul be fitted to have God reveal Himself; the deeper we enter into the truth "that no flesh glory in His presence," will it be given us to see His glory. "The eye of the Lord is on them that fear Him."

"On them that hope in His mercy." So far will the true fear of God be from keeping us back from hope, it will stimulate and strengthen it. The lower we bow, the deeper we feel we have nothing to hope in but His mercy. The lower we bow, the nearer God will come, and make our hearts bold to trust Him. Let every exercise of waiting, let our whole habit of waiting on God, be pervaded[47] by abounding hope—a hope as bright and boundless as God's mercy. The fatherly kindness of God is such that, in whatever state we come to Him, we may confidently hope in His mercy.

Such are God's waiting ones. And now, think of the God on whom we wait. "The eye of the Lord is on them that fear Him, on them that hope in His mercy; to deliver their soul from death, and to keep them alive in famine." Not to prevent the danger of death and famine—this is often needed to stir up to wait on Him—but to deliver and to keep alive. For the dangers are often very real and dark; the situation, whether in the temporal[48] or spiritual life, may appear to be utterly hopeless; there is always one hope: God's eye is on them.

That eye sees the danger, and sees in tender love His trembling waiting child, and sees the moment when the heart is ripe for the blessing, and sees the way in which it is to come. This living, mighty God, oh, let us fear Him and hope in His mercy. And let us humbly but boldly say, "Our soul waiteth for the Lord; He is our help and our shield. Let Thy mercy be upon us, O Lord, according as we wait for Thee."

Oh, the blessedness of waiting on such a God! a very present help in every time of trouble; a shield and defense against every danger. Children of God! will you not learn to sink down in entire helplessness and impotence, and in stillness to wait and see the salvation of God? In the utmost spiritual famine, and when death appears to

47 **Pervaded:** To spread thoroughly and be evident in every part of.

48 **Temporal:** Related to worldly rather than spiritual issues and affairs.

prevail, oh, wait on God. He does deliver, He does keep alive. Say it not only in solitude, but say it to each other—the psalm speaks not of one but of God's people—"Our soul waits on the Lord: He is our help and our shield." Strengthen and encourage each other in the holy exercise of waiting, that each may not only say it of himself, but of his brethren, "We have waited for Him; we will be glad and rejoice in His salvation."

"My soul, wait thou only upon God!"

WAITING ON GOD:
PATIENTLY

Rest in the Lord, and wait patiently for Him.
Those that wait upon the Lord, they shall
inherit the land.

PSALM 37:7, 9 (R.V.)

"IN patience possess your souls."[49] "Ye have need of patience."[50] "Let patience have its perfect work, that ye may be perfect and entire."[51] Such words of the Holy Spirit show us what an important element in the Christian life and character patience is. And nowhere is there a better place for cultivating or displaying it than in waiting on God. There we discover how impatient we are, and what our impatience means. We confess at times that we are impatient with men and circumstances that hinder us, or with ourselves and our slow progress in the Christian life. If we truly set ourselves to wait upon God, we shall find that it is with Him we are impatient, because He does not at once, or as soon as we could wish, do our bidding. It is in waiting upon God that our eyes are opened to believe in His wise and sovereign will, and to see that the sooner and the more completely we

49 "In patience possess...":
Luke 21:19.

50 "Ye have need...":
Hebrews 10:36.

51 "Let patience have...":
James 1:4.

yield absolutely to it, the more surely His blessing can come to us.

"It is not of him that wills, nor of him that runs, but of God that shows mercy."[52] We have as little power to increase or strengthen our spiritual life, as we had to originate it. We "were born not of the will of the flesh, nor of the will of man, but of the will of God."[53] Even so, our willing and running, our desire and effort, avail nought; all is "of God that showeth mercy." All the exercises of the spiritual life, our reading and praying, our willing and doing, have their very great value. But they can go no farther than this, that they point the way and prepare us in humility to look to and to depend alone upon God Himself, and in patience to await His good time and mercy. The waiting is to teach us our absolute dependence upon God's mighty working, and to make us in perfect patience place ourselves at His disposal. They that wait on the Lord shall inherit the land; the promised land and its blessing. The heirs must wait; they can afford to wait.

"Rest in the lord, and wait patiently for Him." The margin gives for "Rest in the Lord," "Be silent to the Lord," or R.V., "Be still before the Lord." It is resting in the Lord, in His will, His promise, His faithfulness, and His love, that makes patience easy. And the resting in Him is nothing but being silent unto Him, still before Him. Having our thoughts and wishes, our fears and hopes, hushed into calm and quiet in that great peace of God which passeth all understanding.[54] That peace keeps the heart and mind when we are anxious for anything, because we have made our request known to Him. The

52   "It is not of him...":
     Romans 9:16.

53   "were born not of...":
     John 1:13.

54   "Peace of God
     which passeth all
     understanding": A
     reference to Philippians
     4:7.

rest, the silence, the stillness, and the patient waiting, all find their strength and joy in God Himself.

The needs be, and the reasonableness, and the blessedness of patience will be opened up to the waiting soul. Our patience will be seen to be the counterpart of God's patience. He longs far more to bless us fully than we can desire it. But, as the husbandman[55] has long patience until the fruit be ripe, so God bows Himself to our slowness and bears long with us. Let us remember this, and wait patiently: of each promise and every answer to prayer the word is true: "I the Lord will hasten it in its time."

55   **Husbandman:** Farmer.

"Rest in the Lord, and wait patiently for Him." Yes, for Him. Seek not only the help, the gift, you need; seek Himself; wait for Him. Give God His glory by resting in Him, by trusting him fully, by waiting patiently for Him. This patience honors Him greatly; it leaves Him, as God on the throne, to do His work; it yields self wholly into His hands. It lets God be God. If your waiting be for some special request, wait patiently. If your waiting be more the exercise of the spiritual life seeking to know and have more of God, wait patiently. Whether it be in the shorter specific periods of waiting, or as the continuous habit of the soul; rest in the Lord, be still before the Lord, and wait patiently. "They that wait on the Lord shall inherit the land."

"My soul, wait thou only upon God!"

WAITING ON GOD: KEEPING HIS WAYS

Wait on the Lord, and keep His way,
And He shalt exalt thee to inherit the land.

PSALM 37:34

*I*F we desire to find a man whom we long to meet, we inquire where the places and the ways are where he is to be found. When waiting on God, we need to be very careful that we keep His ways; out of these we never can expect to find Him. "Thou meetest him that rejoices and worketh righteousness; those that remember Thee in Thy ways."[56] We may be sure that God is never and nowhere to be found but in His ways. And that there, by the soul who seeks and patiently waits, He is always most surely to be found. "Wait on the Lord, and keep His ways, and He shall exalt thee."

How close the connection between the two parts of the injunction.[57] "Wait on the Lord,"—that has to do with worship and disposition; "and keep His ways,"—that deals with walk and work. The outer life must be in harmony with the inner; the inner must be the inspiration and the strength for the outer. It is our God who has made known His ways in His Word for our conduct, and invites our

56   "Thou meetest him...":
Isaiah 64:5.

57   **Injunction:** A warning or direct order, typically from one who's in authority.

confidence for His grace and help in our heart. If we do not keep His ways, our waiting on Him can bring no blessing. The surrender to a full obedience to all His will, is the secret of full access to all the blessings of His fellowship.

Notice how strongly this comes out in the psalm. It speaks of the evildoer who prospers in his way, and calls on the believer not to fret himself. When we see men around us prosperous and happy while they forsake God's ways, and ourselves left in difficulty or suffering, we are in danger of first fretting at what appears so strange, and then gradually yielding to seek our prosperity in their path. The psalm says, "Fret not thyself; trust in the Lord, and do good. Rest in the Lord, and wait patiently for Him; cease from anger, and forsake wrath. Depart from evil, and do good; the Lord forsakes not His saints. The righteous shall inherit the land. The law of his God is in his heart; none of his steps shall slide."[58] And then follows—the word occurs for the third time in the psalm—"Wait on the Lord, and keep His ways." Do what God asks you to do; God will do more than you can ask Him to do.

And let no one give way to the fear: I cannot keep His ways; it is this robs us of our confidence. It is true you have not the strength yet to keep all His ways. But keep carefully those for which you have received strength already. Surrender yourself willingly and trustingly to keep all God's ways, in the strength which will come in waiting on Him. Give up your whole being to God without reserve and without doubt; He will prove Himself God to you, and work in you that which is pleasing in His sight through Jesus Christ. Keep His ways, as you know

58 A mash up of verses from Psalm 37 (verses 1, 3, 7-8, 27-29, and 31).

them in the Word. Keep His ways, as nature teaches them, in always doing what appears right. Keep His ways, as Providence[59] points them out. Keep His ways, as the Holy Spirit suggests. Do not think of waiting on God while you say you are not willing to walk in His path. However weak you feel, only be willing, and He who has worked to will, will work to do by His power.

"Wait on the Lord, and keep His ways." It may be that the consciousness of shortcoming and sin makes our text look more like a hindrance than a help in waiting on God. Let it not be so. Have we not said more than once, the very starting-point and groundwork of this waiting is utter and absolute impotence? Why then not come with everything evil you feel in yourself, every memory of unwillingness, unwatchfulness, unfaithfulness, and all that causes such unceasing self condemnation? Put your trust in God's omnipotence,[60] and find in waiting on God your deliverance. Your failure has been owing to only one thing: you sought to conquer and obey in your own strength. Come and bow before God until you learn that He is the God who alone is good, and alone can work any good thing. Believe that in you, and all that nature can do, there is no true power. Be content to receive from God each moment the inworking of His mighty grace and life, and waiting on God will become the renewal of your strength to run in His ways and not be weary, to walk in His paths and never faint. "Wait on the Lord, and keep His ways" will be command and promise in one.

"My soul, wait thou only upon God!"

59   **Providence:** In this use, God and His direction.

60   **Omnipotence:** Unlimited or exceedingly great power.

THIRTEENTH DAY

WAITING ON GOD:
FOR MORE THAN WE KNOW

And now, Lord, what wait I for? My hope is in Thee. Deliver me from all my transgressions.

PSALM 39:7, 8

*T*HERE may be times when we feel as if we knew not what we are waiting for. There may be other times when we think we do know, and when it would just be so good for us to realize that we do not know what to ask as we ought. God is able to do for us exceeding abundantly above what we ask or think, and we are in danger of limiting Him, when we confine our desires and prayers to our own thoughts of them. It is a great thing at times to say, as our psalm says: "And now, Lord, what wait I for?" I scarce know or can tell; this only I can say—"My hope is in Thee."

How we see this limiting of God in the case of Israel! When Moses promised them meat in the wilderness, they doubted, saying, "Can God furnish a table in the wilderness? He smote the rock that the water gushed out; can He give bread also? Can He provide flesh for His people?"[61] If they had been asked whether God could

61   "Can God furnish...":
     Psalm 78:19-20.

provide streams in the desert, they would have answered, Yes. God had done it: He could do it again. But when the thought came of God doing something new, they limited Him; their expectation could not rise beyond their past experience, or their own thoughts of what was possible. Even so we may be limiting God by our conceptions of what He has promised or is able to do. Do let us beware of limiting the Holy One of Israel in our very prayer. Let us believe that every promise of God we plead has a divine meaning, infinitely beyond our thoughts of them. Let us believe that His fulfilment of them can be, in a power and an abundance of grace, beyond our largest grasp of thought. And let us therefore cultivate the habit of waiting on God, not only for what we think we need, but for all His grace and power are ready to do for us.

In every true prayer there are two hearts in exercise. The one is your heart, with its little, dark, human thoughts of what you need and God can do. The other is God's great heart, with its infinite, its divine purposes of blessing. What think you? To which of these two ought the larger place to be given in your approach to Him? Undoubtedly, to the heart of God: everything depends upon knowing and being occupied with that. But how little this is done. This is what waiting on God is meant to teach you. Just think of God's wonderful love and redemption, in the meaning these words must have to Him. Confess how little you understand what God is willing to do for you, and say each time as you pray "And now, what wait I for?" My heart cannot say. God's heart knows and waits to give. "My hope is in Thee." Wait on God to do for you more than you can ask or think.

Apply this to the prayer that follows: "Deliver me from all my transgressions." You have prayed to be delivered from temper, or pride, or self-will. It is as if it is in vain. May it not be that you have had your own thoughts about the way or the extent of God's doing it, and have never waited on the God of glory, according to the riches of His glory, to do for you what has not entered the heart of man to conceive?[62] Learn to worship God as the God who does wonders, who wishes to prove in you that He can do something supernatural and divine. Bow before Him, wait upon Him, until your soul realizes that you are in the hands of a divine and almighty worker. Consent not to know what and how He will work; expect it to be something altogether godlike, something to be waited for in deep humility, and received only by His divine power. Let the, "And now, Lord, what wait I for? My hope is in Thee" become the spirit of every longing and every prayer. He will in His time do His work.

Dear soul, in waiting on God you may often be ready to be weary, because you hardly know what you have to expect. I pray you, be of good courage—this ignorance is often one of the best signs. He is teaching you to leave all in His hands, and to wait on Him alone. "Wait on the Lord! Be strong, and let your heart take courage. Yea, wait on the Lord."[63]

"My soul, wait thou only upon God!"

62   **Conceive:** Imagine.

63   "Wait on the Lord! Be strong...": Psalm 27.14.

WAITING ON GOD:
THE WAY TO THE NEW SONG

> I waited patiently for the Lord,
> and He inclined unto me, and heard my cry. . . .
> And He hath put a new song in my mouth,
> even praise unto our God.
>
> **PSALM 40: 1-3**

*C*OME and listen to the testimony of one who can speak from experience of the sure and blessed outcome of patient waiting upon God. True patience is so foreign to our self-confident nature, it is so indispensable in our waiting upon God, it is such an essential element of true faith, that we may well once again meditate on what the word has to teach us.

The word patience is derived from the Latin word for suffering.[64] It suggests the thought of being under the constraint of some power from which we want to be free. At first we submit against our will; experience teaches us that when it is vain to resist, patient endurance is our wisest course. In waiting on God it is of infinite consequence that we not only submit, because we are compelled to, but because we lovingly and joyfully consent to be in the hands of our blessed Father. Patience then becomes

64 **Suffere** (Latin root of suffer): To endure or bear.

our highest blessedness and our highest grace. It honors God, and gives Him time to have His way with us. It is the highest expression of our faith in His goodness and faithfulness. It brings the soul perfect rest in the assurance that God is carrying on His work. It is the token of our full consent[65] that God should deal with us in such a way and time as He thinks best. True patience is the losing of our self-will in His perfect will.

Such patience is needed for the true and full waiting on God. Such patience is the growth and fruit of our first lessons in the school of waiting. To many a one it will appear strange how difficult it is truly to wait upon God. The great stillness of soul before God that sinks into its own helplessness and waits for Him to reveal Himself; the deep humility that is afraid to let its own will or its own strength work aught except as God works to will and to do; the meekness that is content to be and to know nothing except as God gives His light; the entire resignation of the will that only wants to be a vessel in which His holy will can move and mold: all these elements of perfect patience are not found at once. But they will come in measure as the soul maintains its position, and ever again says: "Truly my soul waiteth upon God; from Him cometh my salvation: He only is my rock and my salvation."[66]

Have you ever noticed what proof we have that patience is a grace for which very special grace is given, in these words of Paul: "Strengthened with all might, according to His glorious power, unto all"—what? "patience and long-suffering with joyfulness."[67] Yes, we need to be strengthened with all God's might, and that

65 "Token of our full consent": A sign, often visible, of our willingness and permission.

66 "Truly my soul...": Psalm 62:1-2.

67 "Strengthened with all might...": Colossians 1:11.

according to the measure of His glorious power, if we are to wait on God in all patience. It is God revealing Himself in us as our life and strength, that will enable us with perfect patience to leave all in His hands. If any are inclined to despond,[68] because they have not such patience, let them be of good courage; it is in the course of our feeble and very imperfect waiting that God Himself by His hidden power strengthens us and works out in us the patience of the saints, the patience of Christ Himself.

Listen to the voice of one who was deeply tried: "I waited patiently for the Lord, and He inclined unto me, and heard my cry." Hear what he passed through: "He brought me up also out of an horrible pit, out of the miry clay, and set my feet upon a rock, and established my goings. And He has put a new song in my mouth, even praise unto our God. Patient waiting upon God brings a rich reward; the deliverance is sure; God Himself will put a new song into your mouth. O soul! be not impatient, whether it be in the exercise of prayer and worship that you find it difficult to wait, or in the delay in respect of definite requests, or in the fulfilling of your heart's desire for the revelation of God Himself in a deeper spiritual life—fear not, but rest in the Lord, and wait patiently for Him. And if you sometimes feel as if patience is not your gift, then remember it is God's gift, and take that prayer (2 Thess. 3:5 R.V.): "The Lord direct your hearts into the patience of Christ." Into the patience with which you are to wait on God, He Himself will guide you.

"My soul, wait thou only upon God!"

68   **Despond:** To lose confidence or become depressed or dejected.

WAITING ON GOD:
FOR HIS COUNSEL

They soon forgot His works:
they waited not for His counsel.

PSALM 106:13

*T*HIS is said of the sin of God's people in the wilderness. He had wonderfully redeemed them, and was prepared as wonderfully to supply their every need. But, when the time of need came, "they waited not for His counsel." They thought not that the Almighty God was their Leader and Provider; they asked not what His plans might be. They simply thought the thoughts of their own heart, and tempted and provoked God by their unbelief. "They waited not for His counsel."

How this has been the sin of God's people in all ages! In the land of Canaan, in the days of Joshua, the only three failures of which we read were owing to this one sin. In going up against Ai, in making a covenant with the Gibeonites, in settling down without going up to possess the whole land, they waited not for His counsel. And so even the advanced believer is in danger from this most subtle of temptations—taking God's word and thinking his own thoughts of them, and not waiting for

69 **Collective capacity**: In this usage, the Church or any individual congregation.

His counsel. Let us take the warning and see what Israel teaches us. And let us very specially regard it not only as a danger to which the individual is exposed, but as one against which God's people, in their collective capacity,[69] need to be on their guard.

Our whole relation to God is rooted in this, that His will is to be done in us and by us as it is in heaven. He has promised to make known His will to us by His Spirit, the Guide into all truth. And our position is to be that of waiting for His counsel, as the only guide of our thoughts and actions. In our church worship, in our prayer-meetings, in our conventions, in all our gatherings as managers, or directors, or committees, or helpers in any part of the work for God, our first object ought ever to be to ascertain the mind of God. God always works according to the counsel of His will; the more that counsel of His will is sought and found and honoured, the more surely and mightily will God do His work for us and through us.

70 **Sound creed:** Theologically solid religious beliefs.

The great danger in all such assemblies is that in our consciousness of having our Bible, and our past experience of God's leading, and our sound creed,[70] and our honest wish to do God's will, we trust in these, and do not realize that with every step we need and may have a heavenly guidance. There may be elements of God's will, applications of God's word, experiences of the close presence and leading of God, manifestations of the power of His Spirit, of which we know nothing as yet. God may be willing, no, God is willing to open up these to the souls who are intently set upon allowing Him to have His way entirely, and who are willing in patience to wait for His making it known. When we come together praising God for all He has done and taught and given, we may at the same time be limiting Him by not expecting greater things. It was when God had given the water out of the rock that they did not trust Him for bread. It was when God had given Jericho into his hands that Joshua thought the victory over Ai was sure; he now knew what God could do, and waited not for counsel from God. And so, while we think that we know and trust the power of God for what we may expect, we may be hindering Him by not giving time, and not definitely cultivating the habit of waiting for His counsel.

A minister has no more solemn duty than teaching people to wait upon God. Why was it that in the house of Cornelius, when "Peter spoke these words, the Holy Ghost fell upon all that heard him"?[71] They had said, "We are here before God to hear all things that are commanded you of God."[72] We may come together to give and to listen to the most earnest exposition of God's truth with little spiritual profit if there be not the waiting for God's counsel. In all our gatherings we need to believe in the Holy Spirit as the Guide and Teacher of God's saints when they wait to be led by Him into the things which God has prepared, and which the heart cannot conceive.

More stillness of soul to realize God's presence; more consciousness of ignorance of what God's great plans may be; more faith in the certainty that God has greater things to show us; more longing that He Himself may be revealed in new glory: these must be the marks of the assemblies of God's saints, if they would avoid the reproach,[73] "They waited not for His counsel."

"My soul, wait thou only upon God!"

71 Peter spoke these words...": Acts 10:44.

72 "We are here...": Acts 10:33.

73 **Reproach:** An expression of disappointment or disapproval.

WAITING ON GOD:
FOR HIS LIGHT IN THE HEART

I wait for the Lord, my soul doth wait,
And in His word do I hope.
My soul waiteth for the Lord
more than they that watch for the morning:
More than they that watch for the morning.

PSALM 130:5, 6

*W*ITH what intense longing the morning light is often waited for. By the mariners in a shipwrecked vessel; by a benighted[74] traveler in a dangerous country; by an army that finds itself surrounded by an enemy. The morning light will show what hope of escape there may be. The morning may bring life and liberty. And so the saints of God in darkness have longed for the light of His countenance, more than watchmen for the morning. They have said, "More than watchmen for the morning, my soul waiteth for the Lord." Can we say that too? Our waiting on God can have no higher object than simply having His light shine on us, and in us, and through us, all the day.

God is Light. God is a Sun. Paul says: "God has shined in our hearts to give the light." What light? "The

74 Benighted: Overtaken by the darkness of night.

light of the glory of God, in the face of Jesus Christ." Just as the sun shines its beautiful, life-giving light on and into our earth, so God shines into our hearts the light of His glory, of His love, in Christ His Son. Our heart is meant to have that light filling and gladdening it all the day. It can have it, because God is our sun, and it is written, "Your sun shall no more go down forever." God's love shines on us without ceasing.

But can we indeed enjoy it all the day? We can. And how can we? Let nature give us the answer. Those beautiful trees and flowers, with all this green grass, what do they do to keep the sun shining on them? They do nothing; they simply bask in the sunshine, when it comes. The sun is millions of miles away, but over all that distance it sends its own light and joy; and the tiniest flower that lifts its little head upwards is met by the same exuberance of light and blessing as flood the widest landscape. We have not to care for the light we need for our day's work; the sun cares, and provides and shines the light around us all the day. We simply count upon it, and receive it, and enjoy it.

The only difference between nature and grace is this, that what the trees and the flowers do unconsciously, as they drink in the blessing of the light, is to be with us a voluntary and a loving acceptance. Faith, simple faith in God's word and love, is to be the opening of the eyes, the opening of the heart, to receive and enjoy the unspeakable glory of His grace. And even as the trees, day by day, and month by month, stand and grow into beauty and fruitfulness, just welcoming whatever sunshine the sun may give, so it is the very highest exercise of our Christian

75   **Abide:** In this context, to
      await and accept.

life just to abide[75] in the light of God, and let it, and let
Him, fill us with the life and the brightness it brings.

And if you ask, but can it really be, that even as
naturally and heartily as I recognize and rejoice in the
beauty of a bright sunny morning, I can rejoice in God's
light all the day? It can, indeed. From my breakfast-table
I look out on a beautiful valley, with trees and vineyards
and mountains. In our spring and autumn months the
light in the morning is exquisite, and almost involuntarily
we say, How beautiful! And the question comes, Is it
only the light of the sun that is to bring such continual
beauty and joy? And is there no provision for the light of
God being just as much an unceasing source of joy and
gladness? There is, indeed, if the soul will but be still and
wait on Him, will only let God shine.

Dear soul! Learn to wait on the Lord, more than
watchers for the morning. All within you may be very
dark; is that not the very best reason for waiting for the
light of God? The first beginnings of light may be just
enough to discover the darkness, and painfully to humble
you on account of sin. Can you not trust the light to expel
the darkness? Do believe it will. Just bow, even now, in
stillness before God, and wait on Him to shine into you.
Say, in humble faith; God is light, infinitely brighter and
more beautiful than that of the sun. God is light. The
Father, the eternal, inaccessible, and incomprehensible
light. The Son, the light concentrated, and embodied, and
manifested. The Spirit, the light entering and dwelling and
shining in our hearts. God is light, and is here shining on
my heart. I have been so occupied with the rushlights[76] of

76   **Rushlights:** A candle
      made from the central
      stalk of a rush dipped in
      grease.

my thoughts and efforts, I have never opened the shutters to let His light in.

Unbelief has kept it out. I bow in faith: God's light is shining into my heart. The God of whom Paul wrote, "God hath shined into our heart,"[77] is my God. What would I think of a sun that could not shine? What shall I think of a God that does not shine? No, God shines! God is light! I will take time, and just be still, and rest in the light of God. My eyes are feeble, and the windows are not clean, but I will wait on the Lord. The light does shine, the light will shine in me, and make me full of light. And I shall learn to walk all the day in the light and joy of God. My soul waits on the Lord, more than watchers for the morning.

"My soul, wait thou only upon God!"

[77] "God hath shined...": 2 Corinthians 4:6.

SEVENTEENTH DAY

WAITING ON GOD:
IN TIMES OF DARKNESS

*I will wait upon the Lord, that hideth His face
from the house of Jacob; and I will look for Him.*

ISAIAH 8:17

*H*ERE we have a servant of God, waiting upon Him, not on behalf of himself, but of his people, from whom God was hiding his face. It suggests to us how our waiting upon God, though it commences with our personal needs, with the desire for the revelation of Himself, or of the answer to personal petitions, need not, may not, stop there. We may be walking in the full light of God's countenance,[78] and God yet be hiding His face from His people around us; far from our being content to think that this is nothing but the just punishment of their sin, or the consequence of their indifference, we are called with tender hearts to think of their sad estate,[79] and to wait on God on their behalf. The privilege of waiting upon God is one that brings great responsibility. Even as Christ, when He entered God's presence, at once used His place of privilege and honor as intercessor, so we, no less, if we know what it is really to enter in and wait upon God,

78   **Countenance:** One's facial expressions, meaning, in this case, to see God clearly and know him well.

79   **Sad estate:** A specific time or condition being experienced.

must use our access for our less favored brethren. "I will wait upon the Lord, who hides His face from the house of Jacob."[80]

You worship with a certain congregation. Possibly there is not the spiritual life or joy either in the preaching or in the fellowship that you could desire. You belong to a Church, with its many congregations. There is so much of error or worldliness, of seeking after human wisdom and culture, of trust in ordinances and observances,[81] that you do not wonder that God hides His face, in many cases, and that there is but little power for conversion or true edification.[82] Then there are branches of Christian work with which you are connected—a Sunday school, a gospel hall,[83] a young men's association, a mission work abroad—in which the feebleness of the Spirit's working appears to indicate that God is hiding His face. You think, too, you know the reason. There is too much trust in men and money; there is too much formality and self-indulgence; there is too little faith and prayer; too little love and humility; too little of the spirit of the crucified Jesus. At times you feel as if things are hopeless; nothing will help.

Do believe that God can help and will help. Let the spirit of the prophet come into you, as you take his words, and set yourself to wait on God, on behalf of His erring children. Instead of the tone of judgment or condemnation, of despondency or despair, realize your calling to wait upon God. If others fail in doing it, give yourself doubly to it. The deeper the darkness, the greater the need of appealing to the one only Deliverer. The greater

80 "House of Jacob": The descendants of Jacob, meaning the children of Israel.

81 **Ordinances and observations:** Religious decrees and rites.

82 **Edification:** The improvement of a person morally.

83 **Gospel hall:** Non-denominational assemblies of Christians that sprang up in communities impacted by the Revival of 1859 in Ireland and Scotland, later appearing in the United States.

the self-confidence around you, that knows not that it is poor and wretched and blind, the more urgent the call on you who profess to see the evil and to have access to Him who alone can help, to be at your post, waiting upon God. As often as you are tempted to complain, or to sigh and say ever afresh: "I will wait on the Lord, who hides His face from the house of Jacob."

There is a still larger circle—the Christian Church throughout the world. Think of Greek, Roman Catholic, and Protestant churches, and the state of the millions that belong to them. Or think only of the Protestant churches with their open Bible and orthodox creeds. How much nominal[84] profession and formality! how much of the rule of the flesh and of man in the very temple of God! And what abundant proof that God does hide His face!

What are those to do who see and mourn this? The first thing to be done is this: "I will wait on the Lord, who hides His face from the house of Jacob." Let us wait on God, in the humble confession of the sins of His people. Let us take time and wait on Him in this exercise. Let us wait on God in tender, loving intercession for all saints, our beloved brethren, however wrong their lives or their teaching may appear. Let us wait on God in faith and expectation, until He shows us that He will hear. Let us wait on God, with the simple offering of ourselves to Himself, and the earnest prayer that He would send us to our brethren. Let us wait on God, and give Him no rest until He make Zion[85] a joy in the earth. Yes, let us rest in the Lord, and wait patiently for Him who now hides His face from so many of His children. And let us say of the

84 **Nominal:** Insignificant, trifling, or insincere.

85 **Zion:** Often used in Scripture as a synonym for Jerusalem or, used in a larger sense, Israel.

lifting up of the light of His countenance we desire for all His people, "I wait for the Lord, my soul doth wait, and my hope is in His word. My soul waits for the Lord, more than the watchers for the morning, the watchers for the morning."[86]

"My soul, wait thou only upon God!"

86   "I wait for the Lord...":
     Psalm 130:5.

WAITING ON GOD:
TO REVEAL HIMSELF

And it shall be said in that day, Lo, this is our
God; we have waited for Him, and He will save
us: THIS IS THE LORD; we have waited for Him,
we will rejoice and be glad in His salvation.

ISAIAH 25:9

*I*N this passage we have two precious thoughts.

The one, that it is the language of God's people
who have been unitedly waiting on Him; the other, that
the fruit of their waiting has been that God has so revealed
Himself, that they could joyfully say, Lo, this is our God:
this is the Lord. The power and the blessing of united
waiting is what we need to learn.

Note the twice repeated, "We have waited for Him."
In some time of trouble the hearts of the people had been
drawn together, and they had, ceasing from all human
hope or help, with one heart set themselves to wait for
their God. Is not this just what we need in our churches
and conventions and prayer-meetings? Is not the need
of the Church and the world great enough to demand
it? Are there not in the Church of Christ evils to which
no human wisdom is equal? Have we not ritualism and

rationalism, formalism and worldliness, robbing the Church of its power? Have we not culture and money and pleasure threatening its spiritual life? Are not the powers of the Church utterly inadequate to cope with the powers of infidelity and iniquity and wretchedness in Christian countries and in heathendom?[87] And is there not in the promise of God, and in the power of the Holy Spirit, a provision made that can meet the need, and give the Church the restful assurance that she is doing all her God expects of her? And would not united waiting upon God for the supply of His Spirit most certainly seem the needed blessing? We cannot doubt it.

The object of a more definite waiting upon God in our gatherings would be very much the same as in personal worship. It would mean a deeper conviction that God must and will do all; a more humble and abiding entrance into our deep helplessness, and the need of entire and unceasing dependence upon Him; a more living consciousness that the essential thing is, giving God His place of honor and of power; a confident expectation that to those who wait on Him, God will, by His Spirit, give the secret of His acceptance and presence, and then, in due time, the revelation of His saving power. The great aim would be to bring every one in a praying and worshipping company under a deep sense of God's presence, so that when they part there will be the consciousness of having met God Himself, of having left every request with Him, and of now waiting in stillness while He works out His salvation.

It is this experience that is indicated in our text. The fulfilment of the words may, at times, be in such striking

87 **Heathendom:** Lands, people, or beliefs "untouched" by the gospel.

88   **Striking interpositions:**
Actions taken by God that
are as visible as they are
forceful so even those
who don't know him can
feel the impact.

89   "We are now here...": Acts
10:33.

interpositions[88] of God's power that all can join in the cry, "Lo, this is our God; this is the Lord!" They may equally become true in spiritual experience, when God's people in their waiting times become so conscious of His presence that in holy awe souls feel, "Lo, this is our God; this is the Lord!" It is this, alas, that is too much missed in our meetings for worship. The godly minister has no more difficult, no more solemn, no more blessed task, than to lead his people out to meet God, and, before ever he preaches, to bring each one into contact with Him. "We are now here in the presence of God"[89]—these words of Cornelius show the way in which Peter's audience was prepared for the coming of the Holy Spirit. Waiting before God, and waiting for God, and waiting on God, are the one condition of God showing His presence.

A company of believers gathered with the one purpose, helping each other by little intervals of silence, to wait on God alone, opening the heart for whatever God may have of new discoveries of evil, of His will, of new openings in work or methods of work, would soon have reason to say, "Lo, this is our God; we have waited for Him, He shall save us: this is the Lord ; we have waited for Him, we will be glad and rejoice in His salvation."

"My soul, wait thou only upon God!"

WAITING ON GOD:
AS A GOD OF JUDGMENT

Yea, in the way of Thy judgments, O Lord, have
we waited for Thee: . . . for when Thy judgments
are on the earth, the inhabitants of the world
learn righteousness.

ISAIAH 26:8, 9

The Lord is a God of judgment:
blessed are all they that wait for Him.

ISAIAH 30:18

*G*OD is a God of mercy and a God of judgment. Mercy
and judgment are ever together in His dealings. In
the flood, in the deliverance of Israel out of Egypt, in the
overthrow of the Canaanites, we ever see mercy in the midst
of judgment. Within the inner circle of His own people, we
see it too: the judgment punishes the sin, while mercy saves
the sinner. Or, rather, mercy saves the sinner, not in spite of,
but by means of, the very judgment that came upon his sin.
In waiting on God, we must beware of forgetting this: as we
wait we must expect Him as a God of judgment.

"In the way of Thy judgments, have we waited for
Thee." That will prove true in our inner experience. If we

are honest in our longing for holiness, in our prayer to be wholly the Lord's, His holy presence will stir up and discover hidden sin, and bring us very low in the bitter conviction of the evil of our nature, its opposition to God's law, its impotence to fulfil that law. The words will come true, "Who may abide the day of His coming, for HE is like a refiner's fire."[90] "O that Thou would come down, as when the melting fire burns!" In great mercy God executes, within the soul, His judgments upon sin, as He makes it feel its wickedness and guilt. Many a one tries to flee from these judgments: the soul that longs for God, and for deliverance from sin, bows under them in humility and in hope. In silence of soul it says, "Arise, O Lord! and let Thine enemies be scattered. In the way of Thy judgments we have waited for Thee."[91]

Let no one who seeks to learn the blessed art of waiting on God, wonder if at first the attempt to wait on Him only discovers more of his sin and darkness. Let no one despair because unconquered sins, or evil thoughts, or great darkness appear to hide God's face. Was not, in His own Beloved Son, the gift and bearer of His mercy on Calvary, the mercy as if hidden and lost in the judgment? Oh, submit, and sink down deep under the judgment of thine every sin: judgment prepares the way, and breaks out in wonderful mercy. It is written, "Thou shalt be redeemed with judgment."[92] Wait on God, in the faith that His tender mercy is working out in you His redemption in the midst of judgment: wait for Him, He will be gracious to thee.

90   "Who may abide...": Malachi 3:2.

91   "Arise, O Lord..." and "In the way...": A mash up of Psalm 68:1 and Isaiah 26:8. Numbers 10:35 also tells us that Moses also said, "Rise up, Lord, and let thine enemies be scattered" ahead of when the ark of the covenant was moved.

92   "Thou shalt be...": Isaiah 1:27.

There is another application still, one of unspeakable solemnity.[93] We are expecting God, in the way of His judgments, to visit this earth: we are waiting for Him. What a thought! We know of these coming judgments; we know that there are tens of thousands of our professing Christians who live on in carelessness, and who, if no change come, must perish under God's hand. Oh, shall we not do our utmost to warn them, to plead with and for them, if God may have mercy on them. If we feel our want of boldness, want of zeal, want of power, shall we not begin to wait on God more definitely and persistently as a God of judgment, asking Him so to reveal Himself in the judgments that are coming on our very friends, that we may be inspired with a new fear of Him and them, and constrained to speak and pray as never yet. Verily, waiting on God is not meant to be a spiritual self-indulgence. Its object is to let God and His holiness, Christ and the love that died on Calvary, the Spirit and fire that burns in heaven and came to earth, get possession of us, to warn and rouse men with the message that we are waiting for God in the way of His judgments. O Christian! prove that you really believe in the God of judgment.

"My soul, wait thou only upon God!"

93 **Solemnity:** Dignified and serious.

TWENTIETH DAY

WAITING ON GOD: WHO WAITS ON US

And therefore will the Lord wait, that He may be gracious unto you; and therefore will He be exalted, that He may have mercy upon you: for the Lord is a God of judgment: blessed are all they that wait for Him.

ISAIAH 30:18

94   **Impulse:** A strong
       motivation to act.

*W*E must not only think of our waiting upon God, but also of what is more wonderful still, of God's waiting upon us. The vision of Him waiting on us, will give new impulse[94] and inspiration to our waiting upon Him. It will give an unspeakable confidence that our waiting cannot be in vain. If He waits for us, then we may be sure that we are more than welcome; that He rejoices to find those He has been seeking for. Let us seek even now, at this moment, in the spirit of lowly waiting on God, to find out something of what it means: "Therefore will the Lord wait, that He may be gracious unto you." We shall accept and echo back the message: "Blessed are all they that wait for Him."

Look up and see the great God upon His throne. He is Love—an unceasing and inexpressible desire to communicate His own goodness and blessedness to all His creatures. He longs and delights to bless. He has inconceivably glorious purposes concerning every one of His children, by the power of His Holy Spirit, to reveal in them His love and power. He waits with all the longings of a father's heart. He waits that He may be gracious unto you. And each time you come to wait upon Him, or seek to maintain in daily life the holy habit of waiting, you may look up and see Him ready to meet you, waiting that He may be gracious unto you. Yes, connect every exercise,[95] every breath of the life of waiting, with faith's vision of your God waiting for you.

And if you ask, how is it, if He waits to be gracious, that even after I come and wait upon Him, He does not give the help I seek, but waits on longer and longer? there is a double answer. The one is this: God is a wise husbandman, "who waits for the precious fruit of the earth, and has long patience for it."[96] He cannot gather the fruit until it is ripe. He knows when we are spiritually ready to receive the blessing to our profit and His glory. Waiting in the sunshine of His love is what will ripen the soul for His blessing. Waiting under the cloud of trial, that breaks in showers of blessing, is as needful. Be assured that if God waits longer than you could wish, it is only to make the blessing doubly precious. God waited four thousand years,[97] until the fulness of time, before He sent His Son: our times are in His hands: He will avenge His elect speedily: He will make haste for our help, and not delay one hour too long.

The other answer points to what has been said before. The giver is more than the gift; God is more than the

95 **Exercise:** In this usage, every activity or effort.

96 "Who waits for the precious...": James 5:7.

97 In Murray's time (born 1828), it was not uncommon for scholars and clergy alike to ascribe to what is sometimes referred to today as "Young Earth creationism," dating the advent of history to around 4000 B.C.

blessing; and our being kept waiting on Him is the only way for our learning to find our life and joy in Himself. Oh, if God's children only knew what a glorious God they have, and what a privilege it is to be linked in fellowship with Himself, then they would rejoice in Him, even when He keeps them waiting. They would learn to understand better than ever; "Therefore will the Lord wait, that He may be gracious unto you." His waiting will be the highest proof of His graciousness.

"Blessed are all they that wait for Him." Queen has her ladies-in-waiting.[98] The position is one of subordination and service, and yet it is considered one of the highest dignity and privilege, because a wise and gracious sovereign makes them companions and friends. What a dignity and blessedness to be attendants-in-waiting on the Everlasting God, ever on the watch for every indication of His will or favor, ever conscious of His nearness, His goodness, and His grace! "The Lord is good to them that wait for Him." "Blessed are all they that wait for Him." Yes, it is blessed when a waiting soul and a waiting God meet each other. God cannot do His work without His and our waiting His time: let waiting be our work, as it is His. And if His waiting be nothing but goodness and graciousness, let ours be nothing but a rejoicing in that goodness, and a confident expectancy of that grace. And let every thought of waiting become to us simply the expression of unmingled[99] and unutterable blessedness, because it brings us to a God who waits that He may make Himself known to us perfectly as the Gracious One.

"My soul, wait thou only upon God!"

98   **Ladies-in-waiting:** Personal assistants to royalty at court.

99   **Unmingled:** pure, not mixed with anything else.

WAITING ON GOD:
THE ALMIGHTY ONE

They that wait on the Lord shall renew their strength; they shall mount up with eagle wings; they shall run and not be weary; they shall walk and not faint.

ISAIAH 40:31

*W*AITING always partakes of the character of our thoughts of the one on whom we wait. Our waiting on God will depend greatly on our faith of what He is. In our text we have the close of a passage in which God reveals Himself as the Everlasting and Almighty One. It is as that revelation enters our soul that the waiting will become the spontaneous expression of what we know Him to be—a God altogether most worthy to be waited upon.

Listen to the words: "Why sayest thou, O Jacob, my way is hid from the Lord?"[100] Why speakest thou as if God does not hear or help? "Hast thou not known, hast thou not heard, that the Everlasting One, the Lord, the Creator of the ends of the earth, fainteth not, neither is weary?" So far from it, "He giveth power to the faint, and to them that have no might He increaseth strength. Even the youths"—"the glory of young men is their strength"—

100 "Why sayest thou...":
Isaiah 40:27-29.

"even the youths shall faint, and the young men shall utterly fall:" all that is accounted strong with man shall come to nought. "But they that wait on the Lord," on the Everlasting One, who does not faint, neither is weary, they "shall renew their strength; they shall mount up with wings as eagles; they shall run and,"—listen now, they shall be strong with the strength of God, and, even as He, "shall not be weary; they shall walk and," even as He, "not faint."

Yes, "they shall mount up with wings as eagles." You know what eagles' wings mean. The eagle is the king of birds, it soars the highest into the heavens. Believers are to live a heavenly life, in the very Presence and Love and Joy of God. They are to live where God lives; they need God's strength to rise there. To them that wait on Him it shall be given.

You know how the eagles' wings are obtained. Only in one way—by the eagle birth. You are born of God. You have the eagles' wings. You may not have known it: you may not have used them; but God can and will teach you to use them.

You know how the eagles are taught the use of their wings. See yonder cliff rising a thousand feet out of the sea. See high up a ledge on the rock, where there is an eagle's nest with its treasure of two young eaglets. See the mother bird come and stir up her nest, and with her beak push the timid birds over the precipice.[101] See how they flutter and fall and sink toward the depth. See now (Deut. 32: 11) "how she fluttereth over her young, spreadeth abroad her wings, taketh them, beareth them on her wings," and

101 **Precipice:** A very high place, especially one that presents a hazardous situation.

so, as they ride upon her wings, brings them to a place of safety. And so she does once and again, each time casting them out over the precipice, and then again taking and carrying them. "So the Lord alone did lead him." Yes, the instinct of that eagle mother was God's gift, a single ray of that love in which the Almighty trains His people to mount as on eagles' wings.

He stirs up your nest. He disappoints your hopes. He brings down your confidence. He makes you fear and tremble, as all your strength fails, and you feel utterly weary and helpless. And all the while He is spreading His strong wings for you to rest your weakness on, and offering His everlasting Creator-strength to work in you. And all He asks is that you should sink down in your weariness and wait on Him; and allow Him in His Jehovah-strength[102] to carry you as you ride upon the wings of His Omnipotence.

102 **Jehovah-strength:** The mighty strength of God.

Dear child of God! I pray you, lift up your eyes, and behold your God! Listen to Him who says that He faints not, neither is weary, who promiseth that you too shall not faint or be weary, who asketh nought but this one thing, that you should wait on Him. And let your answer be, With such a God, so mighty, so faithful, so tender,

"My soul, wait thou only upon God!"

WAITING ON GOD:
IT CERTAINTY OF BLESSING

Thou shalt know that I am the Lord; for they
shall not be ashamed that wait for Me.

ISAIAH 49:23

Blessed are all they that wait for Him.

ISAIAH 30:18

*W*HAT promises! How God seeks to draw us to waiting on Him by the most positive assurance that it never can be in vain: "They shall not be ashamed that wait for Me." How strange that, though we should so often have experienced it, we are yet so slow of learning that this blessed waiting must and can be as the very breath of our life, a continuous resting in God's presence and His love, an unceasing yielding of ourselves for Him to perfect His work in us. Let us once again listen and meditate, until our heart says with new conviction: "Blessed are they that wait for Him!" In our sixth day's lesson we found in the prayer of Psalm 25: "Let none that wait on Thee be ashamed." The very prayer shows how we fear lest it might be. Let us listen to God's answer, until every fear is banished, and we send back to heaven the words God speaks, Yes, Lord, we believe what You say: "All they that wait for Me shall not be ashamed." "Blessed are all they that wait for Him."

The context of each of these two passages points us to times when God's Church was in great straits,[103] and to human eye there was no possibility of deliverance. But God interposes with His word of promise, and pledges His Almighty Power for the deliverance of His people. And it is as the God who has Himself undertaken the work of their redemption, that He invites them to wait on Him, and assures them that disappointment is impossible. We, too, are living in days in which there is much in the state of the Church, with its profession and its formalism, that is indescribably sad. Amid all we praise God for, there is, alas, much to mourn over! Were it not for God's promises we might well despair. But in His promises the Living God has given and bound Himself to us. He calls us to wait on Him. He assureth us we shall not be put to shame. Oh that our hearts might learn to wait before Him, until He Himself reveals to us what His promises mean, and in the promises reveals Himself in His hidden glory! We shall be irresistibly drawn to wait on Him alone. God increase the company of those who say, "Our soul waiteth for the Lord: He is our Help and our Shield."[104]

This waiting upon God on behalf of His Church and people will depend greatly upon the place that waiting on Him has taken in our personal life. The mind may often have beautiful visions of what God has promised to do, and the lips may speak of them in stirring words, but these are not really the measure of our faith or power.

103 **Great straits:** A large amount of trouble.

104 "Our soul waiteth..." Psalm 33:20.

No; it is what we really know of God in our personal experience, conquering the enemies within, reigning and ruling, revealing Himself in His Holiness and Power in our inmost being, —it is this will be the real measure of the spiritual blessing we expect from Him, and bring to our fellowmen. It is as we know how blessed the waiting on God has become to our own souls, that we shall confidently hope in the blessing to come on the Church around us, and the key-word[105] of all our expectations will be; He hath said: "All they that wait on Me shall not be ashamed." From what He has done in us, we shall trust Him to do mighty things around us. "Blessed are all they that wait for Him." Yes, blessed even now in the waiting. The promised blessings, for ourselves, or for others, may tarry; the unutterable blessedness of knowing and having Him who has promised, the Divine Blesser, the Living Fountain of the coming blessings, is even now ours. Do let this truth get full possession of your souls, that waiting on God is itself the highest privilege of the creature, the highest blessedness of His redeemed child.

Even as the sunshine enters with its light and warmth, with its beauty and blessing, into every little blade of grass that rises upward out of the cold earth, so the Everlasting God meets, in the greatness and the tenderness of His love, each waiting child, to shine in his heart "the light of the knowledge of the glory of God in the face of Jesus Christ."[106] Read these words again, until your heart learns to know what God waits to do to you. Who can measure the difference between the great sun and that little blade of grass? And yet the grass has all of

105 **Key-word:** The word or words that unlock or sum up the meaning of a sentence or passage.

106 "The light of the knowledge...": 2 Corinthians 4:6.

the sun it can need or hold. Do believe that in waiting on God, His greatness and your littleness suit and meet each other most wonderfully. Just how in emptiness and poverty and utter impotence, in humility and meekness and surrender to His will, before His great glory, and be still. As you wait on Him, God draws near. He will reveal Himself as the God who will fulfil mightily His every promise. And let your heart ever again take up the song: "Blessed are all they that wait for Him."

"My soul, wait thou only upon God!"

WAITING ON GOD:
FOR UNLOOKED-FOR THINGS

For since the beginning of the world men have
not heard, nor perceived by the ear, neither
hath the eye seen, O God, beside Thee, what He
hath prepared for him that waiteth for Him.

ISAIAH 64:4

THE R.V.[107] has: "Neither hath the eye seen a God beside Thee, which worketh for him that waiteth for Him." In the A.V.[108] the thought is, that no eye hath seen the thing which God hath prepared. In the R.V. no eye hath seen a God, beside our God, who worketh for him that waiteth for Him. To both the two thoughts are common: that our place is to wait upon God, and that there will be revealed to us what the human heart cannot conceive. The difference is: in the R.V. it is the God who works, in the A.V. the thing He is to work. In 1 Cor. 2:9, the citation is in regard to the things which the Holy Spirit is to reveal, as in the A.V., and in this meditation we keep to that.

The previous verses, specially from chap. 63:15, refer to the low state of God's people. The prayer has been poured out, "Look down from heaven." (ver. 15.) "Why

107 R.V.: Though a popular acronym for "recreational vehicles," in this instance, it refers to the "Revised Version" of the Bible. The R.V., sometimes also referred to as the English Revised Version, was commissioned and sanctioned in Britain as a modern update to the King James Version. The R.V. was published in full in 1885.

108 A.V.: The "Authorized Version" of the Bible—the King James Version (KJV). Published in 1611, it became the dominant English language translation through the Twentieth Century.

hast Thou hardened my heart from Thy fear? Return for Thy servants' sake." (ver. 19.) And 64:1, still more urgent, "Oh that Thou wouldest rend the heavens, that thou wouldest come down, . . . as when the melting fire burneth, to make Thy name known to Thy adversaries!" Then follows the plea from the past, When Thou didst terrible things we looked not for, Thou camest down, the mountains flowed down at Thy presence."[109] "For"—this is now the faith that has been awakened by the thought of things we looked not for, He is still the same God— "eye hath not seen beside Thee, O God, what He hath prepared for him that waiteth for Him." God alone knows what He can do for His waiting people. As Paul expounds and applies it: "The things of God knoweth no man, save the Spirit of God. But God hath revealed them to us by His Spirit."[110]

The need of God's people, and the call for God's interposition, is as urgent in our days as it was in the time of Isaiah. There is now, as there was then, as there has been at all times, a remnant that seek after God with their whole heart. But if we look at Christendom as a whole, at the state of the Church of Christ, there is infinite cause for beseeching God to rend the heavens and come down. Nothing but a special interposition of Almighty Power will avail. I fear we have no right conception of what the so-called Christian world is in the sight of God. Unless God comes down "as the melting fire burneth, to make known His name to His adversaries," our labors are comparatively fruitless. Look at the ministry—how much it is in the wisdom of man and of literary culture—

109 "as when the melting fire..." and "When Thou didst...": Isaiah 64:2, 3.

110 "The things of God...": In reference to 1 Corinthians 2:11, 12.

how little in demonstration of the Spirit and of power. Think of the unity of the body—how little there is of the manifestation of the power of a heavenly love binding God's children into one. Think of holiness—the holiness of Christ-like humility and crucifixion to the world—how little the world sees that they have men among them who live in Christ in heaven, in whom Christ and heaven live.

What is to be done? There is but one thing. We must wait upon God. And what for? We must cry, with a cry that never rests, "Oh that Thou wouldest rend the heavens and come down, that the mountains might flow down at Thy presence." We must desire and believe, we must ask and expect, that God will do unlooked-for things. We must set our faith on a God of whom men do not know what He has prepared for them that wait for Him. The wonder-doing God, who can surpass all our expectations, must be the God of our confidence.

Yes, let God's people enlarge their hearts to wait on a God able to do exceeding abundantly above what we can ask or think. Let us band ourselves together as His elect who cry day and night to Him for things men have not seen. He is able to arise and to make His people a name, and a praise in the earth. "He will wait, that He may be gracious unto you; blessed are all they that wait for Him."

"My soul, wait thou only upon God!"

WAITING ON GOD:
TO KNOW HIS GOODNESS

The Lord is good unto them that wait for Him.
LAMENTATIONS 3:25

"THERE is none good but God."[111] "His goodness is in the heavens."[112] "Oh how great is Thy goodness, which Thou hast laid up for them that fear Thee"[113] "Oh, taste and see that the Lord is good!"[114] And here is now the true way of entering into and rejoicing in this goodness of God—waiting upon Him. The Lord is good—even His children often do not know it, for they wait not in quietness for Him to reveal it. But to those who persevere in waiting, whose souls do wait, it will come true. One might think that it is just those who have to wait who might doubt it. But this is only when they do not wait, but grow impatient. The truly waiting ones will all have to say, "The Lord is good to them that wait for Him." Wouldst thou fully know the goodness of God, give thyself more than ever to a life of waiting on Him.

At our first entrance into the school of waiting upon God, the heart is chiefly set upon the blessings which we wait for. God graciously uses our need and desire for help

111 "There is none good...": Matthew 19:16.

112 "His goodness is...:" Psalm 103:11.

113 "Oh how great is...": Psalm 31:19.

114 "Oh, taste and see...": Psalm 34:8.

to educate us for something higher than we were thinking of. We were seeking gifts; He, the Giver, longs to give Himself and to satisfy the soul with His goodness. It is just for this reason that He often withholds the gifts, and that the time of waiting is made so long. He is all the time seeking to win the heart of His child for Himself. He wishes that we should not only say, when He bestows the gift, How good is God! but that long ere it comes, and even if it never comes, we should all the time be experiencing: "It is good that a man should quietly wait":[115] "The Lord is good to them that wait for Him."

115 "It is good that...":
     Lamentations 3:26.

What a blessed life the life of waiting then becomes, the continual worship of faith, adoring and trusting His goodness. As the soul learns its secret, every act or exercise of waiting just becomes a quiet entering into the goodness of God, to let it do its blessed work and satisfy our every need. And every experience of God's goodness gives the work of waiting new attractiveness, and instead of only taking refuge in time of need, there comes a great longing to wait continually and all the day. And however duties and engagements occupy the time and the mind, the soul gets more familiar with the secret art of always waiting. Waiting becomes the habit and disposition, the very second nature and breath of the soul.

Dear Christian! do you not begin to see that waiting is not one among a number of Christian virtues, to be thought of from time to time, but that it expresses that disposition which lies at the very root of the Christian life? It gives a higher value and a new power to our prayer and worship, to our faith and surrender, because it links us, in unalterable dependence, to God Himself. And it gives us the unbroken enjoyment of the goodness of God: "The Lord is good to them that wait for Him."

Let me press upon you once again to take time and trouble to cultivate this so much needed element of the Christian life. We get too much of religion at second hand from the teaching of men. That teaching has great value if, even as the preaching of John the Baptist sent his disciples away from himself to the Living Christ, it leads us to God Himself. What our religion needs is—more of God. Many of us are too much occupied with our work. As with Martha,[116] the very service we want to render the Master separates from Him; it is neither pleasing to Him nor profitable to ourselves. The more work, the more need of waiting upon God; the doing of God's will would then, instead of exhausting, be our meat and drink, nourishment and refreshment and strength. "The Lord is good to them that wait for Him." How good none can tell but those who prove it in waiting on Him. How good none can fully tell but those who have proved Him to the utmost.

"My soul, wait thou only upon God!"

116 "As with Martha:" A reference to Jesus' conversation with Martha found in Luke 10:38-42.

WAITING ON GOD: QUIETLY

It is good that a man should both hope and quietly wait for the salvation of the Lord.
Lamentations 3:26

"TAKE heed, and be quiet: fear not, neither be faint-hearted."[117] "In quietness and in confidence shall be your strength."[118] Such words reveal to us the close connection between quietness and faith, and show us what a deep need there is of quietness, as an element of true waiting upon God. If we are to have our whole heart turned towards God, we must have it turned away from the creature,[119] from all that occupies and interests, whether of joy or sorrow.

God is a being of such infinite greatness and glory, and our nature has become so estranged[120] from Him, that it needs our whole heart and desires set upon Him, even in some little measure to know and receive Him. Everything that is not God, that excites our fears, or stirs our efforts, or awakens our hopes, or makes us glad, hinders us in our perfect waiting on Him. The message is one of deep meaning: "Take heed and be quiet;" "In quietness shall be your strength;" "It is good that a man should quietly wait."

117 "Take heed, and be quiet...": Isaiah 7:4.

118 "In quietness and in...": Isaiah 30:15.

119 **Creature:** In this usage, anything temporary or worldly.

120 **Estranged:** Separated.

How the very thought of God in His majesty and holiness should silence us, Scripture abundantly testifies.

"The Lord is in His holy temple; let all the earth keep silence before Him" (Hab. 2: 20).

"Hold thy peace at the presence of the Lord God." (Zeph. 1:7).

"Be silent, O all flesh, before the Lord; for He is raised up out of His holy habitation" (Zech. 2:13).

As long as the waiting on God is chiefly regarded as an end towards more effectual prayer, and the obtaining of our petitions, this spirit of perfect quietness will not be obtained. But when it is seen that the waiting on God is itself an unspeakable blessedness, one of the highest forms of fellowship with the Holy One, the adoration of Him in His glory will of necessity humble the soul into a holy stillness, making way for God to speak and reveal Himself. Then it comes to the fulfilment of the precious promise, that all of self and self-effort shall be humbled: "The haughtiness of man shall be brought down, and the Lord alone shall be exalted in that day."[121]

121 "The haughtiness of man…": Isaiah 2:17.

Let everyone who would learn the art of waiting on God remember the lesson: "Take heed, and be quiet;" "It is good that a man quietly wait." Take time to be separate from all friends and all duties, all cares and all joys; time to be still and quiet before God. Take time not only to secure stillness from man and the world, but from self and its energy. Let the Word and prayer be very precious; but remember, even these may hinder the quiet waiting. The activity of the mind in studying the Word, or giving expression to its thoughts in prayer, the activities of the

122 **Prostate:** Standing before, especially while bowing.

heart, with its desires and hopes and fears, may so engage us that we do not come to the still waiting on the All-Glorious One; our whole being is not prostrate[122] in silence before Him. Though at first it may appear difficult to know how thus quietly to wait, with the activities of mind and heart for a time subdued, every effort after it will be rewarded; we shall find that it grows upon us, and the little season of silent worship will bring a peace and a rest that give a blessing not only in prayer, but all the day.

"It is good that a man should quietly wait for the salvation of the Lord." Yes, it is good. The quietness is the confession of our impotence, that with all our willing and running, with all our thinking and praying, it will not be done: we must receive it from God. It is the confession of our trust that our God will in His time come to our help—the quiet resting in Him alone. It is the confession of our desire to sink into our nothingness, and to let Him work and reveal Himself. Do let us wait quietly. In daily life let there be in the soul that is waiting for the great God to do His wondrous work, a quiet reverence, an abiding

123 **Engrossment:** Being deeply occupied with or absorbed by.

124 **Beautiful stamp:** A pleasing and distinctive character or resemblance.

watching against too deep engrossment[123] with the world, and the whole character will come to bear the beautiful stamp:[124] Quietly waiting for the salvation of God.

"My soul, wait thou only upon God!"

TWENTY-SIXTH DAY

WAITING ON GOD:
IN HOLY EXPECTANCY

Therefore will I look to the Lord; I will wait for
the God of my salvation; my God will hear me.

MICAH 7:7

*H*AVE you ever read a beautiful little book, Expectation Corner?[125] If not, get it; you will find in it one of the best sermons on our text. It tells of a king who prepared a city for some of his poor subjects. Not far from them were large storehouses, where everything they could need was supplied if they but sent in their requests. But on one condition—that they should be on the outlook for the answer, so that when the king's messengers came with the gifts they had desired, they should always be found waiting and ready to receive them. The sad story is told of one desponding one who never expected to get what he asked, because he was too unworthy. One day he was taken to the king's storehouses, and there, to his amazement, he saw, with his address on them, all the packages that had been made up for him, and sent. There was the garment of praise, and the oil of joy, and the eye salve, and so much more; they had been to his door, but

125 *Expectation Corner*
by Emily Steele Elliott
(1828).

found it closed; he was not on the outlook. From that
time on he understood the lesson Micah would teach us
today; "I will look to the Lord; I will wait for the God of
my salvation; my God will hear me."

We have more than once said: Waiting for the answer
to prayer is not the whole of waiting, but only a part.
Today we want to take in the blessed truth: It is a part, and
a very important one. When we have special petitions,[126]
in connection with which we are waiting on God, our
waiting must be very definitely in the confident assurance:
"My God will hear me." A holy, joyful expectancy is of the
very essence of true waiting. And this not only in reference
to the many varied requests every believer has to make,
but most especially to the one great petition which ought
to be the chief thing every heart seeks for itself—that The
Life of God in the soul may have full sway; that Christ may
be fully formed within; and that we may be filled to all the
fullness of God. This is what God has promised. This is
what God's people too little seek, very often because they
do not believe it possible. This is what we ought to seek
and dare to expect, because God is able and waiting to
work it in us.

But God Himself must work it. And for this end our
working must cease. We must see how entirely it is to be
the faith of the operation of God who raised Jesus from
the dead—just as much as the resurrection, the perfecting
of God's life in our souls is to be directly His work. And
waiting has to become more than ever a tarrying[127] before
God in stillness of soul, counting upon Him who raises the
dead, and calls the things that are not as though they were.

126 **Special petitions:**
     Specific prayers.

127 **Tarrying:** Delaying, in
     this case, a deliberate
     waiting before God.

Just notice how the threefold use of the name of God in our text points us to Himself as the one from whom alone is our expectation. "I will look to The Lord; I will wait for The God of my Salvation; My God will hear me." Everything that is salvation, everything that is good and holy, must be the direct mighty work of God Himself within us. For every moment of a life in the will of God, there must be the immediate operation of God. And the one thing I have to do is this: to look to the Lord; to wait for the God of my salvation; to hold fast the confident assurance, "My God will hear me."

God says: "Be still, and know that I am God."[128]

128 "Be still…": Psalm 46:10.

There is no stillness like that of the grave. In the grave of Jesus, in the fellowship of His death, in death to self with its own will and wisdom, its own strength and energy, there is rest. As we cease from self, and our soul becomes still to God, God will arise and show Himself. "Be still, and know," then you shall know "that I am God." There is no stillness like the stillness Jesus gives when He speaks, "Peace, be still."[129] In Christ, in His death, and in His life, in His perfected redemption, the soul may be still, and God will come in, and take possession, and do His perfect work.

129 "Peace, be still": Mark 4:39.

"My soul, wait thou only upon God!"

TWENTY-SEVENTH DAY

WAITING ON GOD:
FOR REDEMPTION

> Simeon was just and devout, waiting for the
> consolation of Israel, and the Holy Ghost was
> upon him. Anna, a prophetess, . . . spake
> of Him to all then that looked for redemption
> in Jerusalem.
>
> **LUKE 2:25, 38**

*H*ERE we have the mark of a waiting believer. Just, righteous in all his conduct; devout, devoted to God, ever walking as in His presence; waiting for the consolation of Israel, looking for the fulfilment of God's promises: and the Holy Ghost was on him. In the devout waiting he had been prepared for the blessing. And Simeon was not the only one. Anna spoke to all that looked for redemption in Jerusalem. This was the one mark, amid surrounding formalism and worldliness, of a godly band of men and women in Jerusalem. They were waiting on God; looking for His promised redemption.

And now that the Consolation of Israel[130] has come, and the redemption has been accomplished, do we still need to wait? We do indeed. But will not our waiting, who look back to it as come, differ greatly from those who

130 "Consolation of Israel": The promised Messiah.

looked forward to it as coming? It will, especially in two aspects. We now wait on God in the full power of the redemption: and we wait for its full revelation.

Our waiting is now in the full power of the redemption. Christ spoke, "In that day you shall know that you are in Me. Abide in Me."[131] The Epistles teach us to present ourselves to God "as indeed dead to sin, and alive to God in Christ Jesus,"[132] "blessed with all spiritual blessings in heavenly places in Christ Jesus."[133] Our waiting on God may now be in the wonderful consciousness, wrought and maintained by the Holy Spirit within us, that we are accepted in the Beloved, that the love that rests on Him rests on us, that we are living in that love, in the very nearness and presence and sight of God. The old saints took their stand on the word of God, and waited, hoping on that word; we rest on the word too—but, oh! under what exceeding greater privileges, as one with Christ Jesus. In our waiting on God, let this be our confidence: in Christ we have access to the Father; how sure, therefore, may we be that our waiting cannot be vain.

Our waiting differs also in this, that while they waited for a redemption to come, we see it accomplished, and now wait for its revelation in us. Christ not only said, Abide in Me, but also I in you. The Epistles not only speak of us in Christ, but of Christ in us, as the highest mystery of redeeming love. As we maintain our place in Christ day by day, God waits to reveal Christ in us, in such a way that He is formed in us, that His mind and disposition[134] and likeness acquire form and substance in us, so that by each it can in truth be said, "Christ liveth in me."[135]

131 "In that day...": John 4:20.

132 "As indeed dead to sin...": Romans 6:11.

133 "Blessed with all...": Ephesians 1:3.

134 **Disposition:** Someone's inherent character and way of thinking.

135 "Christ liveth in me": Galatians 2:20.

My life in Christ up there in heaven and Christ's life in me down here on earth—these two are the complement of each other. And the more my waiting on God is marked by the living faith I in Christ, the more the heart thirsts for and claims the CHRIST IN ME. And the waiting on God, which began with special needs and prayer, will increasingly be concentrated, as far as our personal life is concerned, on this one thing, Lord, reveal Your redemption fully in me; let Christ live in me.

Our waiting differs from that of the old saints in the place we take, and the expectations we entertain. But at root it is the same: waiting on God, from whom alone is our expectation.

Learn from Simeon and Anna one lesson. How utterly impossible it was for them to do anything towards the great redemption—towards the birth of Christ or His death. It was God's work. They could do nothing but wait. Are we as absolutely helpless as regards the revelation of Christ in us? We are indeed. God did not work out the great redemption in Christ as a whole, and leave its application in detail to us.

The secret thought that it is so lies at the root of all our feebleness. The revelation of Christ in every individual believer, and in each one the daily revelation, step by step and moment by moment, is as much the work of God's omnipotence as the birth or resurrection of Christ. Until this truth enters and fills us, and we feel that we are just as dependent upon God for each moment of our life in the enjoyment of redemption as they were in their waiting for it, our waiting upon God will not bring its full blessing. The sense of utter and absolute helplessness, the confidence that God can and will do all, —these must be the marks of our waiting as of theirs. As gloriously as God proved Himself to them the faithful and wonder-working God, He will to us also.

"My soul, wait thou only upon God!"

WAITING ON GOD:
FOR THE COMING
OF HIS SON

Be ye yourselves like unto men
that wait for their Lord.

LUKE 3:36

Until the appearing of our Lord Jesus Christ,
which, in His own time, He shall shew, who is
the blessed and only Potentate, the King of
kings, and Lord of lords.

1 TIMOTHY 6:14, 15 (R.V.)

Turned to God from idols to serve the living and
true God, and to wait for His Son from heaven.

1 THESSALONIANS 1:9, 10

WAITING on God in heaven, and waiting for His Son from heaven, these two God has joined together, and no man may put them asunder. The waiting on God for His presence and power in daily life will be the only true preparation for waiting for Christ in humility and true holiness. The waiting for Christ coming from heaven to take us to heaven will give the waiting on God its true tone of hopefulness and joy. The Father who in

His own time will reveal His Son from heaven, is the God who, as we wait on Him, prepares us for the revelation of His Son. The present life and the coming glory are inseparably connected in God and in us.

There is sometimes a danger of separating them. It is always easier to be engaged with the religion of the past or the future than to be faithful in the religion of today. As we look to what God has done in the past, or will do in time to come, the personal claim of present duty and present submission to His working may be escaped. Waiting on God must ever lead to waiting for Christ as the glorious consummation[136] of His work; and waiting for Christ must ever remind us of the duty of waiting upon God, as our only proof that the waiting for Christ is in spirit and in truth. There is such a danger of our being so occupied with the things that are coming more than with Him who is to come; there is such scope in the study of coming events for imagination and reason and human ingenuity, that nothing but deeply humble waiting on God can save us from mistaking the interest and pleasure of intellectual study for the true love of Him and His appearing. All ye that say ye wait for Christ's coming, be sure that you wait on God now. All ye that seek to wait on God now to reveal His Son in you, see to it that ye do so as men waiting for the revelation of His Son from heaven. The hope of that glorious appearing will strengthen you in waiting upon God for what He is to do in you now: the same omnipotent love that is to reveal that glory is working in you even now to fit you for it.

136 **Consummation:** Completion.

137 "The blessed hope...":
Titus 2:13.

138 **Bonds of union:**
Connections that unite.

139 "He shall come to be...": 2
Thessalonians 1:10.

"The blessed hope and the appearing of the glory of our great God and Savior Jesus Christ,"[137] is one of the great bonds of union[138] given to God's Church throughout the ages. "He shall come to be glorified in His saints, and to be marveled at in all them that believe."[139] Then we shall all meet, and the unity of the body of Christ be seen in its divine glory. It will be the meeting-place and the triumph of divine love. Jesus receiving His own and presenting them to the Father. His own meeting Him and worshiping in speechless love that blessed face. His own meeting each other in the ecstasy of God's own love. Let us wait, long for, and love the appearing of our Lord and Heavenly Bridegroom. Tender love to Him and tender love to each other is the true and only bridal spirit.

I fear greatly that this is sometimes forgotten. A beloved brother in Holland was speaking about the expectancy of faith being the true sign of the bride. I ventured to express a doubt. An unworthy bride, about to be married to a prince, might only be thinking of the position and the riches that she was to receive. The expectancy of faith might be strong, and true love utterly wanting. It is love in the bridal spirit. It is not when we are most occupied with prophetic subjects, but when in humility and love we are clinging close to our Lord and His brethren, that we are in the bride's place. Jesus refuses to accept our love except as it is love to His disciples. Waiting for His coming means waiting for the glorious coming manifestation of the unity of the body, while we seek here to maintain that unity in humility and love. Those who love most are the most ready for His coming.

Love to each other is the life and beauty of His bride, the Church.

And how is this to be brought about? Beloved child of God! if you would learn aright[140] to wait for His Son from heaven, live even now waiting on God in heaven. Remember how Jesus lived ever waiting on God. He could do nothing of Himself. It was God who perfected His Son through suffering and then exalted Him. It is God alone who can give you the deep spiritual life of one who is really waiting for His Son: wait on God for it. Waiting for Christ Himself is, oh, so different from waiting for things that may come to pass! The latter any Christian can do; the former, God must work in you every day by His Holy Spirit. Therefore all you who wait on God, look to Him for grace to wait for His Son from heaven in the Spirit which is from heaven. And you who would wait for His Son, wait on God continually to reveal Christ in you.

The revelation of Christ in us as it is given to them who wait upon God is the true preparation for the full revelation of Christ in glory.

"My soul, wait thou only upon God!"

140 **Aright:** Properly or correctly.

WAITING ON GOD: FOR THE PROMISE OF THE FATHER

He charged them not to depart from Jerusalem,
but to wait for the promise of the Father.

ACTS 1:4

*I*N speaking of the saints in Jerusalem at Christ's birth, with Simeon and Anna, we saw how, though the redemption they waited for is come, the call to waiting is no less urgent now than it was then. We wait for the full revelation in us of what came to them, but what they scarce could comprehend. Even so it is with waiting for the promise of the Father. In one sense, the fulfillment can never come again as it came at Pentecost. In another sense, and that in as deep reality as with the first disciples, we daily need to wait for the Father to fulfil His promise in us.

The Holy Spirit is not a person distinct from the Father in the way two persons on earth are distinct. The Father and the Spirit are never without or separate from each other: the Father is always in the Spirit; the Spirit works nothing but as the Father works in Him. Each moment the same Spirit that is in us, is in God too, and he who is most full of the Spirit will be the first to wait on God most earnestly, further to fulfil His promise, and still strengthen him mightily by His Spirit in the inner man. The Spirit in us is not a power at our disposal. Nor is the Spirit an independent power, acting apart from the Father and the Son. The Spirit is the real living presence and the power of the Father working in us, and therefore it is just he who knows that the Spirit is in him, who will wait on the Father for the full revelation and experience of what the Spirit's indwelling is, for His increase and abounding more and more.

See this in the apostles. They were filled with the Spirit at Pentecost. When they, not long after, on returning from the Council,[141] where they had been forbidden to preach, prayed afresh for boldness to speak in His name—a fresh coming down of the Holy Spirit was the Father's fresh fulfilment of His promise.

At Samaria, by the word and the Spirit, many had been converted, and the whole city filled with joy. At the apostles' prayer the Father once again fulfilled the promise. Even so to the waiting company—"We are all here before God"—in Cornelius' house. And so, too, in Acts 13. It was when men, filled with the Spirit, prayed and fasted, that the promise of the Father was afresh fulfilled, and the leading of the Spirit was given from heaven: "Separate Me Barnabas and Saul."[142]

So also we find Paul in Ephesians, praying for those who have been sealed with the Spirit, that God would grant them the spirit of illumination. And later on, that He would grant them, according to the riches of His glory,

141 "Returning from the Council…": A reference to the appearance of Peter and John before the High Priest and other rulers following Jesus' resurrection. See Acts 4.

142 "Separate Me…": Acts 13:2

to be strengthened with might by the Spirit in the inner man.

The Spirit given at Pentecost was not a something that God parted with in heaven, and sent away out of heaven to earth. God does not, cannot, give away anything in that way. When He gives grace, or strength, or life, He gives it by giving Himself to work it—it is all inseparable from Himself. (See note on Law, The Power of the Spirit, at the end of this volume.)[143] Much more so is the Holy Spirit. He is God, present and working in us: the true position in which we can count upon that working with an unceasing power is as we, praising for what we have, still unceasingly wait for the Father's promise to be still more mightily fulfilled.

What new meaning and promise does this give to our life of waiting! It teaches us ever to keep the place where the disciples tarried at the footstool of the Throne. It reminds us that, as helpless as they were to meet their enemies, or to preach to Christ's enemies, until they were endued[144] with power, we, too, can only be strong in the life of faith, or the work of love, as we are in direct communication with God and Christ, and they maintain the life of the Spirit in us. It assures us that the Omnipotent God will, through the glorified Christ, work in us a power that can bring to pass things unexpected, things impossible. Oh! what will not the Church be able to do when her individual members learn to live their lives waiting on God, and when together, with all of self and the world sacrificed in the fire of love, they unite in waiting with one accord for the promise of the Father,

143 A reference to an author, William Law, and to Murray's *Author Notes,* which follow the Day 31 reading.

144 **Endued:** Provided with.

once so gloriously fulfilled, but still unexhausted.

Come and let each of us be still in presence of the inconceivable grandeur of this prospect: the Father waiting to fill the Church with the Holy Ghost. And willing to fill me, let each one say.

With this faith let there come over the soul a hush and a holy fear, as it waits in stillness to take it all in. And let life increasingly become a deep joy in the hope of the ever fuller fulfilment of the Father's promise.

"My soul, wait thou only upon God!"

THIRTIETH DAY

WAITING ON GOD: CONTINUALLY

Therefore turn thou to thy God: keep mercy and
judgment, and wait on thy God continually.

HOSEA 12:6

145 **Continuity:** The
consistent, steady,
unbroken existence of a
process or operation.

CONTINUITY[145] is one of the essential elements of
life. Interrupt it for a single hour in a man, and it
is lost, he is dead. Continuity, unbroken and ceaseless,
is essential to a healthy Christian life. God wants me to
be, and God waits to make me, I want to be, and I wait
on Him to make me, every moment, what He expects of
me, and what is well-pleasing in His sight. If waiting on
God be of the essence of true religion, the maintenance
of the spirit of entire dependence must be continuous.
The call of God, "Wait on your God continually," must
be accepted and obeyed. There may be times of special
waiting: the disposition and habit of soul must be there
unchangeably and uninterrupted.

This waiting continually is indeed a necessity. To
those who are content with a feeble Christian life, it
appears a luxury something beyond what is essential
to being a good Christian. But all who are praying the

prayer, "Lord! make me as holy as a pardoned sinner can be made! Keep me as near to Thee as it is possible for me to be! Fill me as full of Thy love as You are willing to do!" Feel at once that it is something that must be had. They feel that there can be no unbroken fellowship with God, no full abiding in Christ, no maintaining of victory over sin and readiness for service, without waiting continually on the Lord.

The waiting continually is a possibility. Many think that with the duties of life it is out of the question. They cannot be always thinking of it. Even when they wish to, they forget.

They do not understand that it is a matter of the heart, and that what the heart is full of, occupies it, even when the thoughts are otherwise engaged. A father's heart may be filled continuously with intense love and longing for a sick wife or child at a distance, even though pressing business requires all his thoughts. When the heart has learned how entirely powerless it is for one moment to keep itself or bring forth any good, when it has understood how surely and truly God will keep it, when it has, in despair of itself, accepted God's promise to do for it the impossible, it learns to rest in God, and in the midst of occupations and temptations it can wait continually.

This waiting is a promise. God's commands are enablings:[146] gospel precepts[147] are all promises, a revelation of what our God will do for us. When first you begin waiting on God, it is with frequent intermission and frequent failure. But do believe God is watching over you in love and secretly strengthening you in it. There are

146 **Enablings:** In this case, a way by which we can receive power to do as commanded.

147 **Precepts:** Instructions and rules meant to guide thought and action.

times when waiting appears to be just losing time, but it is not so. Waiting, even in darkness, is unconscious advance, because it is God you have to do with, and He is working in you. God who calls you to wait on Him, sees your feeble efforts, and works it in you. Your spiritual life is in no respect your own work: as little as you began it, can you continue it; it is God's Spirit who has begun the work in you of waiting upon God; He will enable you to wait continually.

Waiting continually will be met and rewarded by God Himself working continually. We are coming to the end of our meditations. Would that you and I might learn one lesson: God must, God will work continually. He ever does work continually, but the experience of it is hindered by unbelief. But He who by His Spirit teaches you to wait continually, will bring you to experience also how, as the Everlasting One, His work is never-ceasing. In the love and the life and the work of God there can be no break, no interruption.

Do not limit God in this by your thoughts of what may be expected. Do fix your eyes upon this one truth: in His very nature, God, as the only Giver of life, cannot do otherwise than every moment work in His child. Do not look only at the one side: "If I wait continually, God will work continually." No, look at the other side. Place God first and say, "God works continually, every moment I may wait on Him continually." Take time until the vision of your God working continually, without one moment's intermission, fill your being. Your waiting continually will then come of itself. Full of trust and joy, the holy habit of the soul will be, "On Thee do I wait all the day."[148] The Holy Spirit will keep you ever waiting.

"My soul, wait thou only upon God!"

MOMENT BY MOMENT[149]

"I the Lord do keep it: I will water it every moment."[150]
Dying with Jesus, by death reckoned mine,
Living with Jesus a new life divine;
Looking to Jesus till glory doth shine,
Moment by moment, O Lord, I am Thine.
Chorus—Moment by moment I'm kept in His love,
Moment by moment I've life from above;
Looking to Jesus till glory doth shine;
Moment by moment, O Lord, I am Thine.
Never a battle with wrong for the right,
Never a contest that He doth not fight;
Lifting above us His banner so white,
Moment by moment I'm kept in His sight.
Chorus

Never a trial that He is not there,
Never a burden that He doth not bear,
Never a sorrow that He does not share,
Moment by moment I'm under His care.
Chorus

Never a heartache, and never a groan,
Never a teardrop, and never a moan;

148 "On Thee do...": Psalm 25:5.

149 This hymn was written by Ira Sankey (1840-1908). He was a singer and composer and in 1980 was inducted into the Gospel Music Hall of Fame.

150 "I the Lord...": Isaiah 27:3

Never a danger but there on the throne
Moment by moment He thinks of His own.
Chorus

Never a weakness that He doth not feel,
Never a sickness that He cannot heal;
Moment by moment, in woo or in weal,
Jesus, my Savior, abides with me still.
Chorus

Music in *Christian Endeavor Hymns* by I. D. Sankey. Or on leaflet by Morgan & Scott.

WAITING ON GOD: ONLY

My soul, wait thou only upon God;
For my expectation is from Him.
He only is my rock and my salvation.

ISAIAH 62:5, 6

*I*T is possible to be waiting continually on God, but not only upon Him; there may be other secret confidences[151] intervening and preventing the blessing that was expected. And so the word *only* must come to throw its light on the path to the fulness and certainty of blessing. "My soul, wait thou only upon God. He only is my Rock."

Yes, "My soul, wait thou only upon God." There is but one God, but one source of life and happiness for the heart; He only is my Rock; my soul, wait thou only upon Him. Thou desirest to be good. "There is none good but God," and there is no possible goodness but what is received directly from Him. Thou hast sought to be holy: "There is none holy but the Lord," and there is no holiness but what He by His Spirit of holiness every moment breathes in thee. Thou wouldest live and work

151 **Secret confidences:**
Used here, a secret reliance on something or someone other than God.

for God and His kingdom, for men and their salvation. Hear how He says, "The Everlasting God, the Creator of the ends of the earth. He "alone" fainteth not, neither is weary. He giveth power to the faint, and to them that have no might He increaseth strength. They that wait upon the Lord shall renew their strength."[152] He only is God; He only is thy Rock: "My soul, wait thou only upon God."

"My soul, wait thou only upon God." Thou will not find many who can help you in this. Enough there will be of thy brethren to draw thee to put trust in churches and doctrines, in schemes and plans and human appliances, in means of grace and divine appointments. But, "My soul, wait thou only upon God Himself." His most sacred appointments[153] become a snare when trusted in. The brazen serpent becomes Nehushtan;[154] the ark and the temple a vain confidence. Let the Living God alone, none and nothing but He, be thy hope.

"My soul, wait thou only upon God." Eyes and hands and feet, mind and thought, may have to be intently engaged in the duties of this life; "My soul, wait thou only upon God." Thou art an immortal spirit, created not for this world but for eternity and for God. O, my soul! Realize thy destiny. Know thy privilege, and "wait thou only upon God." Let not the interest of religious thoughts and exercises deceive you; they very often take the place of waiting upon God. My soul, wait thou, thy very self, your inmost being, with all its power, "wait thou only upon God." God is for thee, thou art for God; wait only upon Him.

Yes, "my soul, wait thou only upon God." Beware of your two great enemies—the World and Self. Beware lest

---

152 "The Everlasting God...": Isaiah 40: 28-29, 31.

153 **Sacred appointments:** Furnishings or equipment dedicated to God.

154 **Nehushtan:** A brazen thing, a piece of brass; as well as the name given in 2 Kings 18:4 to the bronze serpent on a pole that Moses had held up in the wilderness (Numbers 21:4-9).

any earthly satisfaction or enjoyment, however innocent it appears, keep you back from saying, "I will go to God, my exceeding joy." Remember and study what Jesus says about denying self, "Let a man deny himself." Tersteegen[155] says: "The saints deny themselves in everything." Pleasing self in little things may be strengthening it to assert itself in greater things. "My soul, wait thou only upon God;" let Him be all your salvation and all your desire. Say continually and with an undivided heart, "From Him comes my expectation; He only is my Rock; I shall not be moved." Whatever be thy spiritual or temporal need, whatever the desire or prayer of thy heart, whatever thy interest in connection with God's work in the Church or the world—in solitude or in the rush of the world, in public worship or other gatherings of the saints, "My soul, wait thou only upon God." Let your expectations be from Him alone. He only is your Rock.

"My soul, wait thou only upon God." Never forget the two foundation-truths on which this blessed waiting rests. If ever you are inclined to think this "waiting only" is too hard or too high, they will recall thee at once. They are: your absolute helplessness; and, the absolute sufficiency of thy God. Oh! enter deep into the entire sinfulness of all that is of self, and think not of letting self have anything to say one single moment. Enter deep into thy utter and unceasing impotence ever to change what is evil in thee, or to bring forth anything that is spiritually good. Enter deep into thy relation of dependence as creature on God, to receive from Him every moment what He gives. Enter deeper still into His covenant of redemption, with His

155 **Gerhard Tersteegen** (1697-1769) was a German hymnist, poet, and writer.

promise to restore more gloriously than ever what thou hadst lost, and by His Son and Spirit to give within you unceasingly, His actual divine Presence and Power. And thus wait upon your God continually and only.

"My soul, wait thou only upon God." No words can tell, no heart conceive, the riches of the glory of this mystery of the Father and of Christ. Our God, in the infinite tenderness and omnipotence of His love, waits to be our Life and Joy. Oh, my soul! let it be no longer needed that I repeat the words, "Wait upon God," but let all that is in me rise and sing: "Truly my soul waits upon God. On Thee do I wait all the day."[156]

"My soul, wait thou only upon God!"[157]

156 "Truly my soul..." and "On Thee do...": Psalm 62:1 and 25:5.

157 Murray ends this book as he began it: Quoting Psalm 62:5, the theme verse of "Waiting for God," which has been repeated in these pages well over 40 times!

AUTHOR NOTES[158]

*M*Y publishers have just issued a work of William Law[159] on the Holy Spirit. [The Power of the Holy Spirit: An humble earnest, and affectionate Address to the Clergy. With Additional Extracts and Introduction, by Rev. Andrew Murray. (Fleming H. Revell Company. $1.00)] In the Introduction I have said how much I owe to the book. I cannot but think that anyone who will take the trouble to read it thoughtfully will find rich spiritual profit in the connection with a life of Waiting upon God.

What he puts more clearly than I have anywhere else found are these cardinal truths:— [160]

1. That the very Nature and Being of a God, as the only Possessor and Dispenser of any life there is in the universe, imply that He must every moment communicate to every creature the power by which it exists, and therefore also much more the power by which it can do that which is good.

2. That the very Nature and Being of a creature, as owing its existence to God alone, and equally owing to Him each moment the continuation of that existence, imply that its happiness can only be found in absolute unceasing momentary dependence upon God.

3. That the great value and blessing of the gift of the Spirit at Pentecost, as the fruit of Christ's Redemption, is that it is now possible for God to take posses of His redeemed children and work in them as He did

158 Separate from the margin notes which have been added to this book as a special feature, these *Author Notes* come from Andrew Murray and were part of the original publication.

159 **William Law** (1686-1761), an English author, entered Emmanuel College, Cambridge, in 1705 but was dismissed from the school when he refused to take an oath of allegiance when George 1 ascended to the British throne.

160 Here Murray freely acknowledges he benefited greatly from William Law's *The Power of the Spirit*, which made an indelible impression upon him.

before that fall in Adam. We need to know the Holy Spirit as the Presence and Power of God in us restored to their true place.

4. That in the spiritual life our great need is the knowledge of two great lessons. The one our entire sinfulness and helplessness—our utter impotence by maintenance and increase of our inner spiritual life. The other, the infinite willingness of God's love, which is nothing but a desire to communicate Himself and His blessedness to us to meet our every need, and every moment to work us in by His Son and Spirit what we need.

5. That, therefore, the very essence of true religion, whether in heaven or upon earth, consists in an unalterable dependence upon God, because we can give God no other glory, than yielding ourselves to His love, which created us to show forth in us the glory, that it may now perfect its work in us.

I need not point out how deep down these truths go to the very root of the spiritual life, and specially the life of Waiting upon God. I am confident that those who are willing to take the trouble of studying this thoughtful writer will thank me for the introduction in his book.

WORKING FOR GOD

Andrew Murray

PREFACE

*T*HE object of this little book is first of all to remind all Christian workers of the greatness and the glory of the work in which God gives a share. It is nothing less than that work of bringing men back to their God, at which God finds His highest glory and blessedness. As we see that it is God's own work we have to work out, that He works it through us, that in our doing it His glory rests on us and we glorify Him, we shall count it our joy to give ourselves to live only and wholly for it.

The aim of the book at the same time is to help those who complain, and perhaps do not even know to complain, that they are apparently labouring in vain, to find out what may be the cause of so much failure. God's work must be done in God's way, and in God's power. It is spiritual work, to be done by spiritual men, in the power of the Spirit. The clearer our insight into, and the more complete our submission to, God's laws of work, the surer and the richer will be our joy and our reward in it.

Along with this I have had in view the great number of Christians who practically take no real part in the service of their Lord. They have never understood that the chief characteristic of the Divine life in God and Christ is love and its work of blessing men. The Divine life in us can show itself in no other way. I have tried to show that it is God's will that every believer without exception, whatever be his position in life, gives himself wholly to live and work for God.

I have also written in the hope that some, who have the training of others in Christian life and work, may find thoughts that will be of use to them in teaching the imperative duty, the urgent need, the Divine blessedness of a life given to God's service, and to waken within the consciousness of the power that works in them, even the Spirit and power of Christ Himself.

To the great host of workers in Church and Chapel, in Mission-Hall[1] and Open-Air,[2] in Day and Sunday Schools, in Endeavour Societies,[3] in Y. M. and Y. W.[4] and Students' Associations, and all the various forms of the ministry of love throughout the world, I lovingly offer these meditations, with the fervent prayer that God, the Great Worker, may make us true Fellow-Workers with Himself.

—ANDREW MURRAY.
Wellington, February, 1901

1 **Mission-Hall:** A building used for gatherings of Christians.

2 **Open-Air:** Christian gatherings that happen outside.

3 **Endeavor Societies:** The Young People's Society of Christian Endeavor was founded in 1881 and became an international organization. The society's goals were to "bring youth to accept Christ and work for Him."

4 **Y.M. and Y.W.:** In this context, likely Young Men's and Young Women's organizations (e.g., such as the YMCA, which started as a Christian ministry—Young Men's Christian Association).

WORKING FOR GOD:
WAITING AND WORKING

They that wait upon the Lord shall renew their
strength. Neither hath the eye seen,
O God, beside Thee, which worketh for him
that waiteth for Him.

ISAIAH 40:31, 64:4[5]

5   In this book, as
in *Waiting on God*,
Scriptures not noted as
"R. V." (Revised Version,
1885) are generally from
the King James Version
or a Murray paraphrase.

*H*ERE we have two texts in which the connection between waiting and working is made clear. In the first we see that waiting brings the needed strength for working—that it fits for joyful and unwearied work. "They that wait on the Lord shall renew their strength; they shall mount up on eagles' wings; they shall run, and not be weary; they shall walk, and not faint." Waiting on God has its value in this: it makes us strong in work for God. The second reveals the secret of this strength. God "worketh for Him that waiteth for Him." The waiting on God secures the working of God for us and in us, out of which our work must spring. The two passages teach the great lesson, that as waiting on God lies at the root of all true working for God, so working for God must be the fruit of all true waiting on Him. Our great need is to hold the two sides of the truth in perfect conjunction and harmony.

There are some who say they wait upon God, but who do not work for Him. For this there may be various reasons. Here is one who confounds true waiting on God (in living direct intercourse[6] with Him as the Living One), and the devotion to Him of the energy of the whole being, with the slothful, helpless waiting that excuses itself from all work until God, by some special impulse, has made work easy. Here is another who waits on God more truly, regarding it as one of the highest exercises of the Christian life, and yet has never understood that at the root of all true waiting there must lie the surrender and the readiness to be wholly fitted for God's use in the service of men. And here is still another who is ready to work as well as wait, but is looking for some great inflow of the Spirit's power to enable him to do mighty works, while he forgets that as a believer he already has the Spirit of Christ dwelling in Him; that more grace is only given to those who are faithful in the little; and that it is only in working that we can be taught by the Spirit how to do the greater works. All such, and all Christians, need to learn that waiting has working for its object, that it is only in working that waiting can attain its full perfection and blessedness. It is as we elevate working for God to its true place, as the highest exercise of spiritual privilege and power, that the absolute need and the divine blessing of waiting on God can be fully known.

On the other hand, there are some, there are many, who work for God, but know little of what it is to wait on

6   **Intercourse:** In this use, and elsewhere in this book, communication or dealings between individuals or groups of people.

Him. They have been led to take up Christian work, under the impulse of natural or religious feeling, at the bidding of a pastor or a society, with but very little sense of what a holy thing it is to work for God. They do not know that God's work can only be done in God's strength, by God Himself working in us. They have never learnt that, just as the Son of God could do nothing of Himself, but that the Father in Him did the work, as He lived in continual dependence before Him, so, and much more, the believer can do nothing but as God works in him. They do not understand that it is only as in utter weakness we depend upon Him, His power can rest on us. And so they have no conception of a continual waiting on God as being one of the first and essential conditions of successful work. And Christ's Church and the world are sufferers to-day, oh, so terribly! not only because so many of its members are not working for God, but because so much working for God is done without waiting on God.

Among the members of the body of Christ there is a great diversity of gifts and operations. Some, who are confined to their homes by reason of sickness or other duties, may have more time for waiting on God than opportunity of direct working for Him. Others, who are overpressed[7] by work, find it very difficult to find time and quiet for waiting on Him. These may mutually supply each other's lack. Let those who have time for waiting on God definitely link themselves to some who are working. Let those who are working as definitely claim the aid of those to whom the special ministry of waiting on God has been entrusted. So will the unity and the health of the

7   **Overpressed:** Overwhelmed or overburdened.

body be maintained. So will those who wait know that the outcome will be power for work, and those who work, that their only strength is the grace obtained by waiting. So will God work for His Church that waits on Him.

Let us pray that as we proceed in these meditations on working for God, the Holy Spirit may show us how sacred and how urgent our calling is to work, how absolute our dependence is upon God's strength to work in us, how sure it is that those who wait on Him shall renew their strength, and how we shall find waiting on God and working for God to be indeed inseparably one.

1. It is only as God works for me, and in me, that I can work for Him.
2. All His work for me is through His life in me.
3. He will most surely work, if I wait on Him.
4. All His working for me, and my waiting on Him, has but one aim, to fit me for His work of saving men.[8]

8 In *Waiting on God*, Murray ends each daily reading with the same Bible verse: Psalm 62:5. In *Working for God*, his signature ending changes to a numbered list—summarizing key points.

WORKING FOR GOD:
GOOD WORKS THE LIGHT
OF THE WORLD

Ye are the light of the world. Let your light
shine before men, that they may see your good
works, and glorify your Father
which is in heaven.

MATTHEW 5:14, 16

A light is always meant for the use of those who are
in darkness, that by it they may see. The sun
lights up the darkness of this world. A lamp is hung in a
room to give it light. The Church of Christ[9] is the light
of men. The God of this world[10] hath blinded their eyes;
Christ's disciples are to shine into their darkness and give
them light. As the rays of light stream forth from the
sun and scatter that light all about, so the good works
of believers are the light that streams out from them to
conquer the surrounding darkness, with its ignorance of
God and estrangement from Him.

What a high and holy place is thus given to our
good works. What power is attributed to them. How
much depends upon them. They are not only the light

9   Murray's reference here
is to the Church broadly;
not a specific group of
churches.

10   **God of this world:** Satan.

and health and joy of our own life, but in every deed the means of bringing lost souls out of darkness into God's marvellous light. They are even more. They not only bless men, but they glorify God, in leading men to know Him as the Author of the grace seen in His children. We propose studying the teaching of Scripture in regard to good works, and specially all work done directly for God and His kingdom. Let us listen to what these words of the Master have to teach us.

The aim of good works—It is, that God may be glorified. You remember how our Lord said to the Father: "I have glorified Thee on the earth, I have finished the work which Thou gavest Me to do."[11] We read more than once of His miracles, that the people glorified God. It was because what He had wrought was manifestly[12] by a Divine power. It is when our good works thus too are something more than the ordinary virtues of refined men, and bear the impress of God upon them, that men will glorify God. They must be the good works of which the Sermon on the Mount[13] is the embodiment—a life of God's children, doing more than others, seeking to be perfect as their Father in heaven is perfect. This glorifying of God by men may not mean conversion, but it is a preparation for it when an impression favourable to God has been made. The works prepare the way for the words, and are an evidence to the reality of the Divine truth that is taught, while without them the world is powerless.

The whole world was made for the glory of God. Christ came to redeem us from sin and bring us back to serve and glorify Him. Believers are placed in the world

11 "I have glorified Thee...": John 17:4.

12 **Manifestly:** Done in a way that's clear and obvious.

13 **Sermon on the Mount:** Matthew 5-7.

with this one object, that they may let their light shine in good works, so as to win men to God. As truly as the light of the sun is meant to lighten the world, the good works of God's children are meant to be the light of those who know and love not God. What need that we form a right conception of what good works are, as bearing the mark of something heavenly and divine, and having a power to compel the admission that God is in them.

The power of good works—Of Christ it is written: "In Him was life, and the life was the light of men."[14] The Divine life gave out a Divine light. Of His disciples Christ said: "If any man follow Me, he shall not walk in darkness, but have the light of life."[15] Christ is our life and light. When it is said to us, Let your light shine, the deepest meaning is, let Christ, who dwells in you, shine. As in the power of His life you do your good works, your light shines out to all who see you. And because Christ in you is your light, your works, however humble and feeble they be, can carry with them a power of Divine conviction. The measure of the Divine power which works them in you will be the measure of the power working in those who see them. Give way, O child of God, to the Life and Light of Christ dwelling in you, and men will see in your good works that for which they will glorify your Father which is in heaven.

The urgent need of good works in believers—As needful as that the sun shines every day, yea, more so, is it that every believer lets his light shine before men. For this we have been created anew in Christ, to hold forth the Word of Life, as lights in the world. Christ needs you

14 "In Him was life...": John 1:4.

15 "If any man follow Me...": John 8:12.

urgently, my brother, to let His light shine through you. Perishing men around you need your light, if they are to find their way to God. God needs you, to let His glory be seen through you. As wholly as a lamp is given up to lighting a room, every believer ought to give himself up to be the light of a dark world.

Let us undertake the study of what working for God is, and what good works are as part of this, with the desire to follow Christ fully, and so to have the light of life shining into our hearts and lives, and from us on all around.

1. "Ye are the light of the world!" The words express the calling of the Church as a whole. The fulfilment of her duty will depend upon the faithfulness with which each individual member loves and lives for those around him.

2. In all our efforts to waken the Church to evangelise the world, our first aim must be to raise the standard of life for the individual believer of the teaching: As truly as a candle only exists with the object of giving light in the darkness, the one object of your existence is to be a light to men.

3. Pray God by His Holy Spirit to reveal it to you that you have nothing to live for but to let the light and love of the life of God shine upon souls.

WORKING FOR GOD:
SON, GO WORK

Son, go work to-day in my vineyard.

MATTHEW 21:28

*T*HE father had two sons. To each he gave the command to go and work in his vineyard. The one went, the other went not. God has given the command and the power to every child of His to work in His vineyard, with the world as the field. The majority of God's children are not working for Him and the world is perishing.

Of all the mysteries that surround us in the world, is not one of the strangest and most incomprehensible this—that after 1800 years the very name of the Son of God should be unknown to the larger half of the human race.

Just consider what this means. To restore the ruin sin had wrought, God, the Almighty Creator, actually sent His own Son to the world to tell men of His love, and to bring them His life and salvation. When Christ made His disciples partakers of that salvation, and the unspeakable joy it brings, it was with the express understanding that they should make it known to others, and so be the lights of the world. He spoke of all who through them should believe, having the same calling. He left the world with the distinct instruction to carry the Gospel to every creature, and teach all nations to observe all that He had commanded. He at the same time gave the definite assurance that all power for this work was in Him, that He would always be with His people, and that by the power of His Holy Spirit they would be able to witness to Him to the ends of the earth. And what do we see now? After 1800 years two-thirds of the human race have scarce heard the name of Jesus. And of the other third, the larger half is still as ignorant as if they had never heard.[16]

Consider again what this means. All these dying millions, whether in Christendom or heathendom, have an interest in Christ and His salvation. They have a right to Him. Their salvation depends on their knowing Him. He could change their lives from sin and wretchedness to holy obedience and heavenly joy. Christ has a right to them. It would make His heart glad to have them come and be blessed in Him. But they and He are dependent on the service of His people to be the connecting link to bring them and Him together. And yet what His people do is as nothing to what needs to be done, to what could be done, to what ought to be done.

Just consider yet once again what this means. What a revelation of the state of the Church. The great majority of those who are counted believers are doing nothing towards making Christ known to their fellow-men. Of the remainder, the majority are doing so little, and that little so ineffectually,[17] by reason of the lack of wholehearted

16   According to Global Frontier Missions, out of a world population of nearly 8 billion, over 3 billion have little or no access to the Gospel. This computes to around 40%, compared to Murray's statistic from the late 1800s of 67%.

17   **Ineffectually:** Without having impact, doing poorly.

devotion, that they can hardly be said to be giving themselves to their Lord's service. And of the remaining portion, who have given themselves and all they have to Christ's service, so many are occupied with the hospital work of teaching the sick and the weakly in the Church, that the strength left free for aggressive work, and going forth to conquer the world, is terribly reduced. And so, with a finished salvation,[18] and a loving Redeemer, and a Church set apart to carry life and blessing to men, the millions are still perishing.

18 **Finished salvation:** The "Finished Work" doctrine arose during early Pentecostal revivals and posits that believers are sanctified—made holy—at the time of their conversion and thereafter can grow in grace.

There can be no question to the Church of more intense and pressing importance than this: What can be done to waken believers to a sense of their holy calling, and to make them see that to work for God, that to offer themselves as instruments through whom God can do His work, ought to be the one aim of their life? The vain complaints that are continually heard of a lack of enthusiasm for God's kingdom on the part of the great majority of Christians, the vain attempts to waken anything like an interest in missions proportionate to their claim,[19] or Christ's claim, make us feel that nothing less is needed than a revival that shall be a revolution, and shall raise even the average Christian to an entirely new type of devotion. No true change can come until the truth is preached and accepted, that the law of the kingdom is: Every believer to live only and wholly for God's service and work.

19 **"Proportionate to their claim":** In this case, our interest in missions being equal to their importance.

The father who called his sons to go and work in his vineyard did not leave it to their choice to do as much or as little as they chose. They lived in his home, they were his children, he counted on what they would give him, their time and strength. This God expects of His children. Until it is understood that each child of God is to give His whole heart to his Father's interest and work, until it is understood that every child of God is to be a worker for God, the evangelisation of the world cannot be accomplished. Let every reader listen, and the Father will say to him personally: "Son, go work in My vineyard."

1. Why is it that stirring appeals on behalf of missions often have so little permanent result? Because the command with its motives is brought to men who have not learned that absolute devotion and immediate obedience to their Lord is of the essence of true salvation.

2. If it is once seen, and confessed, that the lack of interest in missions is the token[20] of a low and sickly Christian life, all who plead for missions will make it their first aim to proclaim the calling of every believer to live wholly for God. Every missionary meeting will be a consecration[21] meeting to seek and surrender to the Holy Spirit's power.

3. The average standard of holiness and devotion cannot be higher abroad than at home, or in the Church at large than in individual believers.

4. Every one cannot go abroad, or give his whole time to direct work; but everyone, whatever his calling or circumstances, can give his whole heart to live for souls and the spread of the kingdom.

20 **Token:** In this context, an indication.

21 **Consecration:** Setting something aside for the worship and service of God.

WORKING FOR GOD: TO EACH ONE HIS WORK

As a man sojourning in another country, having given authority to his servants, to each one his work, commanded the porter also to watch.

MARK 13:34

*W*HAT I have said in a previous chapter of the failure of the Church to do her Master's work, or even clearly to insist upon the duty of its being done by every member has often led me to ask the question, What must be done to arouse the Church to a right sense of her calling? This little book is an attempt to give the answer. Working for God must take a very different and much more definite place in our teaching and training of Christ's disciples than it has done.

In studying the question I have been very much helped by the life and writings of a great educationist.[22] The opening sentence of the preface to his biography tells us: "Edward Thring[23] was unquestionably the most original and striking figure in the schoolmaster world of his time in England." He himself attributes his own power and success to the prominence he gave to a few simple principles, and the faithfulness with which he carried

22 **Educationalist:** An expert in the theory and practice of education.

23 **Edward Thring** (1821-1887): This British schoolmaster's changes at the Uppingham School influenced public education throughout England.

them out at any sacrifice. I have found them as suggestive in regard to the work of preaching as of teaching, and to state them will help to make plain some of the chief lessons this book is meant to teach.

The root-principle that distinguished his teaching from what was current at the time was this: Every boy in school, the dullest,[24] must have the same attention as the cleverest. At Eton,[25] where he had been educated, and had come out First,[26] he had seen the evil of the opposite system. The school kept up its name by training a number of men for the highest prizes, while the majority were neglected. He maintained that this was dishonest: there could be no truth in a school which did not care for all alike. Every boy had some gift; every boy needed special attention; every boy could, with care and patience, be fitted to know and fulfil his mission in life.

Apply this to the Church. Every believer, the feeblest as much as the strongest, has the calling to live and work for the kingdom of his Lord. Every believer has equally a claim on the grace and power of the Holy Spirit, according to his gifts, to fit him for his work. And every believer has a right to be taught and helped by the Church for the service our Lord expects of him. It is when this truth, every believer the feeblest, to be trained as a worker for God, gets its true place, that there can be any thought of the Church fulfilling its mission. Not one can be missed, because the Master gave to every one his work.

Another of Thring's principles was this: It is a law of nature that work is pleasure. See to make it voluntary and not compulsory. Do not lead the boys blindfold.[27]

24   **Dullest:** Least bright, slowest to understand.

25   **Eton:** Founded in 1440, Eton College is a public boys-only boarding school, sometimes referred to as "the nurse of England's statesmen," claiming many former Prime Ministers and other leading officials as alumni.

26   **First:** In this usage, First Class Honors (indicating high academic achievement).

27   **Blindfold:** In this context, insisting on behavior without explaining why it's needed.

Show them why they have to work, what its value will be, what interest can be awakened in it, what pleasure may be found in it. A little time stolen, as he says, for that purpose, from the ordinary teaching, will be more than compensated for by the spirit which will be thrown into the work.

What a field is opened out here for the preacher of the gospel in the charge he has of Christ's disciples. To unfold before them the greatness, the glory, the Divine. blessedness of the work to be done. To show its value in the carrying out of God's will, and gaining His approval; in our becoming the benefactors and saviours of the perishing; in developing that spiritual vigour, that nobility of character, that spirit of self-sacrifice which leads to the true bearing of Christ's image.

A third truth Thring insisted on specially was the need of inspiring the belief in the possibility, yea, the assurance of success in gaining the object of pursuit. That object is not much knowledge; not every boy can attain to this. The drawing out and cultivation of the power there is in himself—this is for every boy—and this alone is true education. As a learner's powers of observation grow under true guidance and teaching and he finds within himself a source of power and pleasure he never knew before, he feels a new self beginning[28] to live, and the world around him gets a new meaning. "He becomes conscious of an infinity of unsuspected glory in the midst of which we go about our daily tasks, becomes lord of an endless kingdom full of light and pleasure and power."

28   **Self-beginning**: Fresh motivation, akin to self-starting.

If this be the law and blessing of a true education, what light is shed on the calling of all teachers and leaders in Christ's Church! The know ye nots of Scripture—that ye are the temple of God—that Christ is in you—that the Holy Spirit dwelleth in you[29]—acquire a new meaning. It tells us that the one thing that needs to be wakened in the hearts of Christians is the faith in the "power that worketh in us." As one comes to see the worth and the glory of the work to be done, as one believes in the possibility of his, too, being able to do that work well; as one learns to trust a Divine energy, the very power and spirit of God working in him; "he will, in the fullest sense become conscious of a new life, with an infinity of unsuspected glory in the midst of which we go about our daily task, and become lord of an endless kingdom full of light and pleasure and power." This is the royal life to which God has called all His people. The true Christian is one who knows God's power working in himself, and finds it his true joy to have the very life of God flow into him, and through him, and out from him to those around.

1. We must learn to believe in the power of littles—of the value of every individual believer. As men are saved one by one, they must be trained one by one for work.

2. We must believe that work for Christ can become as natural, as much an attraction and a pleasure in the spiritual as in the natural world.

3. We must believe and teach that every believer can become an effective worker in his sphere.[30] Are you seeking to be filled with love to souls?

29 Murray's "Know ye nots": In reference to 1 Corinthians 3:16 (for "temple of God" and "Spirit dwelleth") and 2 Corinthians 13:5 for "Christ in you."

30 "His sphere": The author is recognizing that individual Christians will serve in their own environments and in their own calling.

WORKING FOR GOD: TO EACH ACCORDING TO HIS ABILITY

The kingdom of heaven is as when a man, going into another country, called his own servants, and delivered them his goods. And unto one he gave five talents, to another two, to another one; to each according to his several ability.

MATTHEW 25:14

31 **Talents:** A considerable sum of money, equal to 3,000 silver shekels.

$\mathcal{I}$N the parable of the talents[31] we have a most instructive summary of our Lord's teaching in regard to the work He has given to His servants to do. He tells us of His going to heaven and leaving His work on earth to the care of His Church; of His giving every one something to do, however different the gifts might be; of His expecting to get back His money with interest; of the failure of him who had received least; and of what it was that led to that terrible neglect.

"He called his own servants and delivered unto them his goods, and went on his journey." This is literally what our Lord did. He went to heaven, leaving His work with all His goods to the care of His Church. His goods were, the riches of His grace, the spiritual blessings in heavenly places, His word and Spirit, with all the power of His life on the throne of God—all these He gave in trust to His servants, to be used by them in carrying out His work on earth. The work He had begun they were to prosecute.[32] As some rich merchant leaves Cape Town to reside in London, while his business is carried on by trustworthy servants, our Lord took His people into partnership with Himself, and entrusted His work on earth entirely to their care. Through their neglect it would suffer; their diligence would be His enrichment. Here we have the true root-principle of Christian service; Christ has made Himself dependent for the extension of His kingdom on the faithfulness of His people.

"Unto one he gave five talents, to another two, to another one; to each according to his several ability."[33] Though there was a difference in the measure, every one received a portion of the master's goods. It is in connection with the service we are to render to each other that we read of "the grace given to each of us according to the measure of the gift of Christ."[34] This truth, that every believer without exception has been set apart to take an active part in the work of winning the world for Christ, has almost been lost sight of. Christ was first a son, then a servant. Every believer is first a child of God, then a servant. It is the highest honour of a son to be a servant, to have the father's work entrusted to him. Neither the home nor the foreign missionary work of the Church will ever be done right until every believer feels that the one object of his being in the world is to work for the kingdom. The first duty of the servants in the parable was to spend their life in caring for their master's interests.

32 **Prosecute:** Continue to completion.

33 **The Parable of the Talents:** Matthew 25:14-30. Murray unpacks various aspects of it in the paragraphs following this reference.

34 "the grace given…": Ephesians 4:7.

"After a long time the lord of those servants cometh and maketh a reckoning with them." Christ keeps watch over the work He has left to be done on earth; His kingdom and glory depend upon it. He will not only hold reckoning when He comes again to judge, but comes unceasingly to inquire of His servants as to their welfare and work. He comes to approve and encourage, to correct and warn. By His word and Spirit He asks us to say whether we are using our talents diligently, and, as His devoted servants, living only and entirely for His work. Some He finds labouring diligently, and to them He frequently says: "Enter into the joy of thy Lord." Others He sees discouraged, and them He inspires with new hope. Some He finds working in their own strength; these He reproves. Still others He finds sleeping or hiding their talent; to such His voice speaks in solemn warning: "from him that hath shall be taken away even that he hath." Christ's heart is in His work; every day He watches over it with the intensest interest; let us not disappoint Him nor deceive ourselves.

"Lord, I was afraid and hid thy talent in the earth." That the man of the one talent should have been the one to fail, and to be so severely punished is a lesson of deep solemnity. It calls the Church to beware lest, by neglecting to teach the feebler ones, the one-talent men, that their service, too, is needed, she allow them to let their gifts lie unused. In teaching the great truth that every branch is to bear fruit, special stress must be laid on the danger of thinking that this can only be expected of the strong and advanced Christian. When Truth reigns in a school, the most backward pupil has the same attention as the more clever. Care must be taken that the feeblest Christians receive special training, so that they, too, may joyfully have their share in the service of their Lord and all the blessedness it brings. If Christ's work is to be done, not one can be missed.

"Lord, I knew that thou art a hard man, and I was afraid." Wrong thoughts of God, looking upon His service as that of a hard master, are one chief cause of failure in service. If the Church is indeed to care for the feeble ones, for the one-talent servants, who are apt to be discouraged by reason of their conscious weakness, we must teach them what God says of the sufficiency of grace and the certainty of success. They must learn to believe that the power of the Holy Spirit within them fits them for the work to which God has called them. They must learn to understand that God Himself will strengthen them with might by His Spirit in the inner man. They must be taught that work is joy and health and strength. Unbelief lies at the root of sloth. Faith opens the eyes to see the blessedness of God's service, the sufficiency of the strength provided, and the rich reward. Let the Church awake to her calling to train the feeblest of her members to know that Christ counts upon every redeemed one to live wholly for His work. This alone is true Christianity, is full salvation.[35]

35 This is the first of only 6 Days (chapters) in *Working for God* that Murray does not close with a numbered list (Days 5, 13, 16, 21, 27 and 30).

WORKING FOR GOD:
LIFE AND WORK

My meat is to do the will of Him that sent Me,
and to accomplish His work. I must work the
works of Him that sent Me. I have glorified
Thee on the earth; I have finished the work
Thou gavest Me to do. And now, O Father,
glorify Me with Thyself.

JOHN 5:34, 9:4, 17:4

"WORK is the highest form of existence." The highest manifestation of the Divine Being is in His work. Read carefully again the words of our Blessed Lord at the head of the chapter, and see what Divine glory there is in His work. In His work Christ showed forth His own glory and that of the Father. It was because of the work He had done, and because in it He had glorified the Father, that He claimed to share the glory of the Father in heaven. The greater works He was to do in answer to the prayer of the disciples was, that the Father might be glorified in the Son. Work is indeed the highest form of existence, the highest manifestation of the Divine glory in the Father and in His Son.

What is true of God is true of His creature. Life is movement, is action, and reveals itself in what it accomplishes. The bodily life, the intellectual, the moral, the spiritual life—individual, social, national life—each of these is judged of by its work. The character and quality of the work depends on the life: as the life, so the work. And, on the other hand the life depends on the work; without this there can be no full development and manifestation and perfecting of the life: as the work, so the life.

This is specially true of the spiritual life—the life of the Spirit in us. There may be a great deal of religious work with its external activities, the outcome of human will and effort, with but little true worth and power, because the Divine life is feeble. When the believer does not know that Christ is living in him, does not know the Spirit and power of God working in him, there may be much earnestness and diligence, with little that lasts for eternity. There may, on the contrary, be much external weakness and apparent failure, and yet results that prove that the life is indeed of God.

The work depends upon the life. And the life depends on the work for its growth and perfection. All life has a destiny; it cannot accomplish its purpose without work; life is perfected by work. The highest manifestation[36] of its hidden nature and power comes out in its work. And so work is the great factor by which the hidden beauty and the Divine possibilities of the Christian life are brought out. Not only for the sake of what it accomplishes through the believer as God's instrument, but what it effects on himself, work must in the child of God take the same

36 **Manifestation:** The disclosing of what was unseen or obscure.

place it has in God Himself. As in the Father and the Son, so with the Holy Spirit dwelling in us, work is the highest manifestation of life.

Work must be restored to its right place in God's scheme of the Christian life as in very deed the highest form of existence. To be the intelligent willing channel of the power of God, to be capable of working the very work of God, to be animated by the Divine Spirit of love, and in that to be allowed to work life and blessing to men; it is this gives nobility to life, because it is for this we are created in the image of God. As God never for a moment ceases to work His work of love and blessing in us and through us, so our working out what He works in us is our highest proof of being created anew in His likeness.

If God's purpose with the perfection of the individual believer, with the appointment of His Church as the body of Christ to carry on His work of winning back a rebellious world to His allegiance and love is to be carried out, working for God must have much greater prominence given to it as the true glory of our Christian calling. Every believer must be taught that, as work is the only perfect manifestation, and therefore the perfection of life in God and throughout the world, so our work is to be our highest glory. Shall it be so in our lives?

If this is to come, we must remember two things. The one is that it can only come by beginning to work. Those who have not had their attention specially directed to it cannot realise how great the temptation is to make work a matter of thought and prayer and purpose, without its really being done. It is easier to bear than to think, easier to think than to speak, easier to speak than to act. We may listen and accept and admire God's will, and in our prayer profess our willingness to do,—and yet not actually do. Let us, with such measure of grace as we have, and much prayer for more, take up our calling as God's working men, and do good hard work for Him. Doing is the best teacher. If you want to know how to do a thing, begin and do it.

Then you will feel the need of the second thing I wish to mention, and be made capable of understanding it—that there is sufficient grace in Christ for all the work you have to do. You will see with ever-increasing gladness how He the Head works all in you the member, and how work for God may become your closest and fullest fellowship with Christ, your highest participation in the power of His risen and glorified life.

1. Life and work: beware of separating them. The more work you have, the more your work appears a failure. The more unfit you feel for work, take all the more time and care to have your inner life renewed in close fellowship with God.

2. "Christ liveth in me"—[37]is the secret of joy and hope, and also of power for work. Care for the life, the life will care for the work. "Be filled with the Spirit."[38]

37 "Christ liveth...": A reference to Galatians 2:20.

38 "Be filled...": Ephesians 5:18.

WORKING FOR GOD:
THE FATHER ABIDING IN ME
DOETH THE WORK

Jesus answered them, My Father worketh
even until now, and I work.

JOHN 5:17-20

Believest thou not that I am in the Father, and
the Father in Me? the words that I speak
I speak not of Myself: but the Father
abiding in Me doeth the work.

JOHN 14:10

JESUS Christ became man that He might show us what a true man is, how God meant to live and work in man,[39] and how man may find his life and do his work in God. In words like those above, our Lord opens up the inner mystery of His life, and discovers to us the nature and the deepest secret of His working. He did not come to the world to work instead of the Father; the Father was ever working—"worketh even until now." Christ's work was the fruit, the earthly reflection of the Heavenly Father working. And it was not as if Christ merely saw and copied what the Father willed or did: "the Father

39   **Work in man:** In this context, mankind. During this time, the equality of the sexes wasn't immediately assumed, and it would have been odd for the author to use the more inclusive "work in people."

abiding in Me doeth the work." Christ did all His work in the power of the Father dwelling and working in Him. So complete and real was His dependence on the Father, that, in expounding it to the Jews, He used the strong expressions (John 5:19, 30): "The Son can do nothing of Himself, but what He seeth the Father doing"; "I can do nothing of Myself." As literally as what He said is true of us, "Apart from Me ye can do nothing,"[40] is it true of Him too. "The Father abiding in Me doeth the work."[41]

40   "Apart from me...": John 15:5.

41   "The Father abiding...": John 14:10.

Jesus Christ became man that He might show us what true man is, what the true relation between man and God, what the true way of serving God and doing His work. When we are made new creatures in Christ Jesus, the life we receive is the very life that was and is in Christ, and it is only by studying His life on earth that we know how we are to live. As I live because of the Father, so "he that eateth Me shall live because of Me."[42] His dependence on the Father is the law of our dependence on Him and on the Father through Him.

42   "he that eateth me...": A reference to Jesus' teaching in John 6:50-57.

Christ counted it no humiliation to be able to do nothing of Himself, to be always and absolutely dependent on the Father. He counted it His highest glory, because so all His works were the works of the all glorious God in Him. When shall we understand that to wait on God, to bow before Him in perfect helplessness, and let Him work all in us, is our true nobility, and the secret of the highest activity? This alone is the true Son-life, the true life of every child of God. As this life is known and maintained, the power for work will grow, because the soul is in the attitude in which God can work in us, as

43   "who worketh...": Isaiah
       64:4.

the God "who worketh for him that waiteth on Him."[43] It is the ignorance or neglect of the great truths, that there can be no true work for God but as God works it in us, and that God cannot work in us fully but as we live in absolute dependence on Him, that is the explanation of the universal complaint of so much Christian activity with so little real result. The revival which many are longing and praying for must begin with this: the return of Christian ministers and workers to their true place before God—in Christ and like Christ, one of complete dependence and continual waiting on God to work in them.

Let me invite all workers, young and old, successful or disappointed, full of hope or full of fear, to come and learn from our Lord Jesus the secret of true work for God. "My Father worketh, and I work;" "The Father abiding in Me doeth the works." Divine Fatherhood means that God is all, and gives all, and works all. Divine Sonship means continual dependence on the Father, and the reception, moment by moment, of all the strength needed for His Work. Try to grasp the great truth that because

44   "God who worketh all in
       all": 1 Corinthians 12:6.

it is "God who worketh all in all,"[44] your one need is, in deep humility and weakness, to wait for and to trust in His working. Learn from this that God can only work in us as He dwells in us. "The Father abiding in Me doeth the works." Cultivate the holy sense of God's continual nearness and presence, of your being His temple, and of His dwelling in you. Offer yourself for Him to work in you all His good pleasure. You will find that work, instead of being a hindrance, can become your greatest incentive to a life of fellowship and childlike dependence.

At first it may appear as if the waiting for God to work will keep you back from your work. It may indeed—but only to bring the greater blessing, when you have learned the lesson of faith, that counts on His working even when you do not feel it. You may have to do your work in weakness and fear and much trembling. You will know that it is all, that the excellency of the power may be of God and not of us. As you know yourself better and God better, you will be content that it should ever be—"His strength made perfect in our weakness."[45]

1. "The Father abiding in Me doeth the work." There is the same law for the Head and the member, for Christ and the believer. It is "the same God that worketh all in all."[46]

2. The Father not only worked in the Son when He was on earth, but now, too, that He is in heaven. It is as we believe in Christ in the Father's working in Him, that we shall do the greater works. See John 14:10-12.

3. It is as the indwelling God, the Father abiding in us, that God works in us. Let the life of God in the soul be clear, the work will be sure.

4. Pray much for grace to say, in the name of Jesus, "The Father abiding in me doeth the work."

45 "His strength made perfect…": 2 Timothy 2:22.

46 "the same God…": I Corinthians 12:6.

WORKING FOR GOD: GREATER WORKS

Verily, verily, I say unto You, He that believeth on Me, the works that I do shall he do also and greater works shall he do; because I go unto the Father. And whatsoever ye shall ask in My name, that will I do, that the Father may be glorified in the Son. If ye shall ask anything in My name, that will I do.

JOHN 14:12-14

*I*N the words (John 14:10) "The Father abiding in Me doeth the works," Christ had revealed the secret of His and of all Divine service—man yielding himself for God to dwell and to work in him. When Christ now promises, "He that believeth on Me, the works that I do shall he do also," the law of the Divine inworking[47] remains unchanged. In us, as much as in Him, one might even say a thousand times more than with Him, it must still ever be: The Father in me doeth the works. With Christ and with us, it is "the same God who worketh all in all."[48]

How this is to be, is taught us in the words, "He that believeth on Me."[49] That does not only mean, for

47 **Inworking:** Something happening within us, in this case, a work of God.

48 "the same God...": 1 Corinthians 12:6.

49 "He that believeth...": John 7:38.

salvation, as a Saviour from sin. But much more. Christ had just said (vers. 10, 11), "Believe Me that I am in the Father, and the Father in Me: the Father abiding in Me doeth the works." We need to believe in Christ as Him in and through whom the Father unceasingly works. To believe in Christ is to receive Him into the heart. When we see the Father's working inseparably connected with Christ, we know that to believe in Christ, and receive Him into the heart, is to receive the Father dwelling in Him and working through Him. The works His disciples are to do cannot possibly be done in any other way than His own are done.

This becomes still more clear from what our Lord adds: "And greater works shall he do; because I go unto the Father." What the greater works are, is evident. The disciples at Pentecost with three thousand baptized, and multitudes added to the Lord; Philip at Samaria, with the whole city filled with joy; the men of Cyprus and Cyrene, and, later on, Barnabas at Antioch, with much people added to the Lord; Paul in his travels, and a countless host of Christ's servants down to our day, have in the ingathering of souls,[50] done what the Master condescendingly calls greater works than He did in the days of His humiliation and weakness.

50 **Ingathering of souls:** Conversions to Christ.

The reason why it should be so our Lord makes plain, "Because I go to the Father." When He entered the glory of the Father, all power in heaven and on earth was given to Him as our Redeemer. In a way more glorious than ever the Father was to work through Him; and He then to work through His disciples. Even as His own work on earth in the days of the weakness of the flesh, had been in a power received from the Father in heaven, so His people, in their weakness, would do works like His, and greater works in the same way, through a power received from heaven. The law of the Divine working is unchangeable: God's work can only be done by God Himself. It is as we see this in Christ, and receive Him in this capacity, as the One in and through whom God works all, and so yield ourselves wholly to the Father working in Him and in us," that we shall do greater works than He did.

The words that follow bring out still more strongly the great truths we have been learning, that it is our Lord Himself who will work all in us, even as the Father did in Him, and that our posture is to be exactly what His was, one of entire receptivity and dependence. "Greater works shall he do, because I go to the Father, and whatsoever ye shall ask in My name, that will I do." Christ connects the greater works the believer is to do, with the promise that He will do whatever the believer asks. Prayer in the name of Jesus will be the expression of that dependence that waits on Him for His working, to which He gives the promise: Whatsoever ye ask, I will do, in you and through you. And when He adds, "that the Father may be glorified in the Son," He reminds us how He had glorified the Father, by yielding to Him as Father, to work all His work in Himself as Son. In heaven Christ would still glorify the Father, by receiving from the Father the power, and working in His disciples what the Father would. The creature, as the Son Himself can give the Father no higher glory than yielding to Him to work all. The believer can glorify the Father in no other way than the Son, by an absolute and unceasing dependence on the Son, in whom the Father works, to communicate and work in us all the Father's work. "If ye shall ask anything in My name, that will I do," and so ye shall do greater works.

Let every believer strive to learn the one blessed lesson. I am to do the works I have seen Christ doing; I may even do greater works as I yield myself to Christ exalted on the throne, in a power He had not on earth; I may count on Him working in me according to that power. My one need is the spirit of dependence and waiting, and prayer and faith, that Christ abiding in me will do the works, even whatsoever I ask.

1. How was Christ able to work the works of God? By God abiding in Him! How can I do the works of Christ? By Christ abiding in me!

2. How can I do greater works than Christ? By believing, not only in Christ, the Incarnate[51] and Crucified, but Christ triumphant on the throne.

    51 **Incarnate:** The union of the divine and human found in Christ Jesus.

3. In work everything depends, O believer, on the life, the inner life, the Divine life. Pray to realise that work is vain except as it is in "the power of the Holy Spirit" dwelling in thee.

WORKING FOR GOD: CREATED IN CHRIST JESUS FOR GOOD WORKS

By grace have ye been saved through faith; not of works, lest any man should glory. For we are His workmanship, created in Christ Jesus for good works, which God afore prepared that we should walk in them.

EPHESIANS 2:8-10

*W*E have been saved, not of works, but for good works. How vast the difference. How essential the apprehension of that difference to the health of the Christian life. Not of works which we have done, as the source whence salvation comes, have we been saved. And yet for good works, as the fruit and outcome of salvation, as part of God's work in us, the one thing for which we have been created anew. As worthless as are our works in procuring salvation, so infinite is their worth as that for which God has created and prepared us. Let us seek to hold these two truths in their fulness of spiritual meaning. The deeper our conviction that we have been saved, not of works, but of grace, the stronger the proof we should give that we have indeed been saved for good works.

"Not of works, for ye are God's workmanship." If works could have saved us, there was no need for our redemption. Because our works were all sinful and vain, God undertook to make us anew—we are now His workmanship, and all the good works we do are His workmanship too. His workmanship, "created us anew in Christ Jesus."[52] So complete had been the ruin of sin, that God had to do the work of creation over again in Christ Jesus. In Him, and specially in His resurrection from the dead, He created us anew, after His own image, into the likeness of the life which Christ had lived. In the power of that life and resurrection, we are able, we are perfectly fitted,[53] for doing good works. As the eye, because it was created for the light, is most perfectly adapted for its work, as the vine-branch, because it was created to bear grapes, does its work so naturally, we who have been created in Christ Jesus for good work, may rest assured that a Divine capacity for good works is the very law of our being. If we but know and believe in this our destiny, if we but live our life in Christ Jesus, as we were new created in Him, we can, we will, be fruitful[54] unto every good work.

Created for good works, which God hath afore prepared that we should walk in them." We have been prepared for the works, and the works prepared for us. To understand this, think of how God foreordained His servants of old, Moses and Joshua, Samuel and David, Peter and Paul, for the work He had for them, and foreordained[55] equally the works for them. The feeblest member of the body is equally cared for by the Head as the most honoured The Father has prepared for the

52   "created us anew...":
      Ephesians 2:10.

53   **Perfectly fitted:** Having
      the appropriate skills and
      abilities.

54   **Fruitful:** In this context,
      producing good, Christ-
      honoring results as we
      labor.

55   **Foreordained:** Appointed
      beforehand.

humblest of His children their works as much as for those who are counted chief. For every child God has a life-plan, with work apportioned[56] just according to the power, and grace provided just according to the work. And so just as strong and clear as the teaching, salvation not of works, is its blessed counterpart, salvation for good works, because God created us for them, and even prepared them for us.

56 **Apportioned:** Allocated.

And so the Scripture confirms the double lesson this little book desires to bring you. The one, that good works are God's object in the new life He has given you, and ought therefore to be as distinctly your object. As every human being was created for work, and endowed with the needful powers, and can only live out a true and healthy life by working, so every believer exists to do good works, that in them his life may be perfected, his fellowmen may be blessed, his Father in heaven be glorified. We educate all our children with the thought that they must have their work in the world: when shall the Church learn that its great work is to train every believer to take his share in God's great work, and to abound in the good works for which he was created? Let each of us seek to take in the deep spiritual truth of the message, "Created in Christ Jesus for good works, which God hath afore prepared" for each one, and which are waiting for him to take up and fulfil.

The other lesson—that waiting on God is the one great thing needed on our part if we would do the good works God has prepared for us. Let us take up into our hearts these words in their Divine meaning: We are God's workmanship. Not by one act in the past, but in a continuous operation. We are created for good works, as the great means for glorifying God. The good works are prepared for each of us, that we might walk in them. Surrender to and dependence upon God's working is our one need. Let us consider how our new creation for good works is all in Christ Jesus, and abiding in Him, believing on Him, and looking for His strength alone will become the habit of our soul. Created for good works! will reveal to us at once the Divine command and the sufficient power to live a life in good works.

Let us pray for the Holy Spirit to work the word into the very depths of our consciousness: Created in Christ Jesus for good works! In its light we shall learn what a glorious destiny, what an infinite obligation, what a perfect capacity is ours.

1. Our creation in Adam was for good works. It resulted in entire failure. Our new creation in Christ is for good works again. But with this difference: perfect provision has been made for securing them.

2. Created by God for good works; created by God in Christ Jesus; the good works prepared by God for us—let us pray for the Holy Spirit to show us and impart to us all this means.

3. Let the life in fellowship with God be true; the power for the work will be sure. As the life, so the work.

WORKING FOR GOD: WORK, FOR GOD WORKS IN YOU

Work out your own salvation with fear and trembling; for it is God which worketh in you both to will and to work, for His good pleasure.

PHILIPPIANS 2:12, 13

*I*N our last chapter we saw what salvation is. It is our being God's workmanship, created in Christ Jesus for good works. It concludes, as one of its chief and essential elements, all that treasury of good works which God afore prepared that we should walk in them. In the light of this thought we get the true and full meaning of to-day's text. Work out your own salvation, such as God has meant it to be, a walk in all the good works which God has prepared for you. Study to know exactly what the salvation is God has prepared for you, all that He has meant and made it possible for you to be, and work it out with fear and trembling. Let the greatness of this Divine and most holy life, hidden in Christ, your own absolute impotence,[57] and the terrible dangers and temptations besetting you, make you work in fear and trembling.

57 **Impotence:** In this context, weakness.

And yet, that fear need never become unbelief, nor that trembling discouragement, for—it is God which worketh in you. Here is the secret of a power that is absolutely sufficient for everything we have to do, of a perfect assurance that we can do all that God really means us to do. God works in us both to will and to work. First, to will; He gives the insight into what is to be done, the desire that makes the work pleasure, the firm purpose of the will that masters the whole being, and makes it ready and eager for action. And then to work. He does not work to will, and then leave us unaided to work it out ourselves. The will may have seen and accepted the work, and yet the power be lacking to perform. The renewed will of Romans 7 delighted in God's law, and yet the man was impotent to do, until in Romans 8:2-4, by the law of the Spirit of life in Christ Jesus, he was set free from the law of sin and death; then first could the righteousness of the law be fulfilled in him, as one who walked not after the flesh but after the Spirit.

One great cause of the failure of believers in their work is that, when they think that God has given them to will, they undertake to work in the strength of that will. They have never learnt the lesson, that because God has created us in Christ Jesus for good works, and has afore prepared the good works in which we are to walk, He must needs, and will most certainly, Himself work them all in us. They have never listened long to the voice speaking, "It is God which worketh in you."

We have here to do with one of the deepest, most spiritual, and most precious truths of Scripture—the unceasing operation of Almighty God in our heart and life. In virtue of the very nature of God, as a Spiritual Being not confined to any place, but everywhere present, there can be no spiritual life but as it is upheld by His personal indwelling.

Not without the deepest reason does Scripture say, He worketh all in all. Not only of Him are all things as their first beginning, and to Him as their end, but also through Him, who alone maintains them.

In the man Christ Jesus the working of the Father in Him was the source of all He did. In the new man, created in Christ Jesus, the unceasing dependence on the Father is our highest privilege, our true nobility. This is indeed fellowship with God: God Himself working in us to will and to do.

Let us seek to learn the true secret of working for God. It is not, as many think, that we do our best, and then leave God to do the rest. By no means. But it is this, that we know that God's working His salvation in us is the secret of our working it out. That salvation includes every work we have to do. The faith of God's working in us is the measure of our fitness to work effectively. The promises, "According to your faith be it unto you,"[58] "All things are possible to him that believeth,"[59] have their full application here. The deeper our faith in God's working in us, the more freely will the power of God work in us, the more true and fruitful will our work be.

Perhaps some Sunday-school worker reads this. Let me ask, Have you really believed that your only power to do God's work is as one who has been created in Christ

58   "According to your faith...": Luke 20:38.

59   "All things are possible...": Matthew 19:26.

Jesus for good works, as one in whom God Himself works to will and to work? Have you yielded yourself to wait for that working? Do you work because you know God works in you? Say not that these thoughts are too high. The work of leading young souls to Christ is too high for us indeed, but if we live as little children, in believing that God will work all in us, we shall do His work in His strength. Pray much to learn and practise the lesson in all you do: Work, for God worketh in you.

1. I think we begin to feel that the spiritual apprehension[60] of this great truth, God worketh in you," is what all workers greatly need.

2. The Holy Spirit is the mighty power of God, dwelling in believers for life and for work. Beseech[61] God to show it you, that in all our service our first care must be the daily renewing of the Holy Spirit.

3. Obey the command to be filled with the Holy Spirit. Believe in His indwelling. Wait for His teaching. Yield to His leading. Pray for His mighty working. Live in the Spirit.

4. What the mighty power of God works in us we are surely able to do. Only give way to the power working in you.

60 **Apprehension:** In this usage, understanding and awareness.

61 **Beseech:** To ask with urgency and fervor.

ELEVENTH DAY

WORKING FOR GOD:
FAITH WORKING BY LOVE

In Christ Jesus neither circumcision availeth anything, nor uncircumcision; but faith working through love. Through love be servants one to another; for the whole law is fulfilled in this: Thou shalt love thy neighbour as thyself.

GALATIANS 5:6, 13

62 **Avails:** Helps or provides benefit.

63 **Token:** A visible representation of a quality or association.

64 **6:15:** In this instance, a reference to Galatians 6:15.

*I*N Christ Jesus no external privilege avails.[62] The Jew might boast of his circumcision, the token[63] of God's covenant. The Gentile might boast of his uncircumcision, with an entrance into the Kingdom free from the Jewish law. Neither availed aught in the Kingdom of heaven—nothing but, as we have it in 6:15,[64] a new creature, in which old things are passed away and all things become new. Or, as we have it in our text—as a description of the life of the new creature—nothing but faith working by love, that makes us in love serve one another.

What a perfect description of the new life. First you have faith, as the root, planted and rooted in Christ Jesus. Then as its aim you have works, as the fruit. And then between the two, as the tree, growing downwards into the root and bearing the fruit upward, you have love, with the life-sap flowing through it by which the root brings forth the fruit, Of faith we need not speak here. We have seen how believing on Jesus does the greater works; how the faith in the new creation, and in God working in us, is the secret of all work. Nor need we speak here of works—our whole book aims at securing for them the place in every heart and life that they have in God's heart and in His Word.

We have here to study specially the great truth that all work is to be love, that faith cannot do its work but through love, that no works can have any worth but as they come of love, and that love alone is the sufficient strength for all the work we have to do.

The power for work is love—It was love that moved God to all His work in creation and redemption. It was love that enabled Christ as man to work and to suffer as He did. It is love that can inspire us with the power of a self-sacrifice that seeks not its own, but is ready to live and die for others. It is love that gives us the patience that refuses to give up the unthankful or the hardened.[65] It is love that reaches and overcomes the most hopeless. Both in ourselves and those for whom we labour love is the power for work. Let us love as Christ loved us.

> 65   **Hardened:** Referring to those whose hearts are unreceptive to God.

The power for love is faith—Faith roots its life in the life of Christ Jesus, which is all love. Faith knows, even when we cannot realise fully, the wonderful gift that has been given into our heart in the Holy Spirit shedding abroad God's love there. A spring in the earth may often be hidden or stopped up. Until. it is opened the fountain cannot flow out. Faith knows that there is a fountain of love within that can spring up into eternal life, that can flow out as rivers of living waters. It assures us that we can love, that we have a Divine power to love within us, as an unalienable endowment of our new nature.

The power to exercise and show love is work—There is no such thing as power in the abstract; it only acts as it is exercised. Power in repose cannot be found or felt. This is specially true of the Christian graces, hidden as they are amid the weakness of our human nature. It is only by doing that you know that you have; a grace must be acted ere we can rejoice in its possession. This is the unspeakable blessedness of work, and makes it so essential to a healthy Christian life that it wakens up and strengthens love, and makes us partakers of its joy.

Faith working by love—In Christ Jesus nothing avails but this. Workers for God! believe this. Practise it. Thank God much for the fountain of eternal love opened within you. Pray fervently and frequently that God may strengthen you with might by the power of His Spirit in your inner man, so that, with Christ dwelling in you, you may be rooted and grounded in love. And live then, your daily life, in your own home, in all your intercourse with men, in all your work, as a life of Divine love. The ways of love are so gentle and heavenly, you may not learn them all at once. But be of good courage, only believe in the power that worketh in you, and yield yourself to the work of love: it will surely gain the victory.

Faith working by love—In Christ Jesus nothing avails but this. Let me press home this message, too, on those who have never yet or only just begun to think of working for God. Come and listen.

You owe everything to God's love. The salvation you have received is all love. God's one desire is to fill you with His love. For His own satisfaction, for your own happiness, for the saving of men. Now, I ask you—Will you not accept God's wonderful offer to be filled with His love? Oh! come and give up heart and life to the joy and the service of His love. Believe that the fountain of love is within you; it will begin to flow as you make a channel for it by deeds of love. Whatever work for God you try to do, seek to put love into it. Pray for the spirit of love. Give yourself to live a life of love; to think how you can love those around you, by praying for them, by serving them, by labouring for their welfare, temporal[66] and spiritual. Faith working by love in Christ Jesus, this alone availeth much.

1. "Faith, Hope, Love: the greatest of these is Love."[67] There is no faith or hope in God. But God is love. The most Godlike thing is love.

2. Love is the nature of God. When it is shed abroad in our hearts by the Holy Spirit love becomes our new nature. Believe this, give yourself over to it, and act it out.

3. Love is God's power to do His work. Love was Christ's power. To work for God pray earnestly to be filled with love to souls!

66 **Temporal:** Of this earth, worldly in nature.

67 "Faith, Hope, Love...": A reference to 1 Corinthians 13:3.

WORKING FOR GOD: BEARING FRUIT IN EVERY GOOD WORK

To walk worthily of the Lord unto all pleasing,
bearing fruit in every good work, and increasing
in the knowledge of God; strengthened with all
power, according to the might of His glory,
unto all patience.

COLOSSIANS 1:10

*T*HERE is a difference between fruit and work. Fruit is that which comes spontaneously, without thought or will, the natural and necessary outcome of a healthy life. Work, on the contrary, is the product of effort guided by intelligent thought and will. In the Christian life we have the two elements in combination. All true work must be fruit, the growth and product of our inner life, the operation of God's Spirit within us. And yet all fruit must be work, the effect of our deliberate purpose and exertion. In the words, "bearing fruit in every good work," we have the practical summing up of the truth taught in some previous chapters. Because God works by His life in us, the work we do is fruit. Because, in the faith of His working, we have to will and to work, the fruit we bear is work. In the harmony between the perfect spontaneity that comes from God's life and Spirit animating us, and our co-operation with Him as His intelligent fellow-labourers, lies the secret of all true work.

In the words that precede our text, "filled with the knowledge of His will in all wisdom and spiritual understanding," we have the human side, our need of knowledge and wisdom; in the words that follow, "strengthened with all power, according to the might of His glory," we have the Divine side. God teaching and strengthening, man learning to understand and patiently do His will; such is the double life that will be fruitful in every good work.

It has been said of the Christian life that the natural man must first become spiritual, and then again the spiritual man must become natural. As the whole natural life becomes truly spiritual, all our work will partake of the nature of fruit, the outgrowth of the life of God within us. And as the spiritual again becomes perfectly natural to us, a second nature in which we are wholly at home, all the fruit will bear the mark of true work, calling into full exercise every faculty of our being.

"Bearing fruit unto every good work." The words suggest again the great thought, that as an apple-tree or a vine is planted solely for its fruit, so the great purpose of our redemption is that God may have us for His work and service. It has been well said: "The end of man is an Action and not a Thought, though it were of the noblest."[68] It is in his work that the nobility of man's nature as ruler of the world is proved. It is for good works that we have been

68 "The end of man is…": A quote from Thomas Carlyle (1795-1881), a Scottish historian and philosopher.

new created in Christ Jesus: It is when men see our good works that our Father in Heaven will be glorified and have the honour which is His due for His workmanship. In the parable of the vine our Lord insisted on this: "He that abideth in Me, and I in him, the same beareth much fruit."[69] "Herein is My Father glorified, that ye bear much fruit."[70] Nothing is more to the honour of a husbandman than to succeed in raising an abundant crop—much fruit is glory to God.

What need that every believer, even the feeblest branch of the Heavenly Vine, the man who has only one talent, be encouraged and helped, and even trained, to aim at the much fruit. A little strawberry plant may, in its measure, be bearing a more abundant crop than a large apple-tree. The call to be fruitful in every good work is for every Christian without exception. The grace that fits for it, of which the prayer, in which our words are found, speaks, is for every one. Every branch fruitful in every good work—this is an essential part of God's Gospel.

"Bearing fruit in every good work." Let us study to get a full impression of the two sides of this Divine truth. God's first creation of life[71] was in the vegetable kingdom. There it was a life without anything of will or self-effort, all growth and fruit was simply His own direct work, the spontaneous outcome of His hidden working. In the creation of the animal kingdom there was an advance. A new element was introduced—thought and will and work. In man these two elements were united in perfect harmony. The absolute dependence of the grass and the lily on the God who clothes them with their beauty were

69   "He that abideth...": John 15:5.

70   "Herein is...": John 15:8.

71   "God's first creation of life": A reference to the Garden of Eden.

to be the groundwork of our relationship—nature has nothing but what it receives from God. Our works are to be fruit, the product of a God-given power. But to this was added the true mark of our God-likeness the power of will and independent action: all fruit is to be our own work. As we grasp this we shall see how the most absolute acknowledgment of our having nothing in ourselves is consistent with the deepest sense of obligation and the strongest will to exert our powers to the very utmost. We shall learn to study the prayer of our text as those who must seek all their wisdom and strength from God alone. And we shall boldly give ourselves, as those who are responsible for the use of that wisdom and strength, to the diligence and the sacrifice and the effort needed for a life bearing fruit in every good work.

1. Much depends, for quality and quantity, on the healthy life of the tree. The life of God, of Christ Jesus, of His Spirit, the Divine life in you, is strong and sure.

2. That life is love. Believe in it. Act it out. Have it replenished day by day out of the fulness there is in Christ.

3. Let all your work be fruit; let all your willing and working be inspired by the life of God. So will you walk worthily of the Lord with all pleasing.

WORKING FOR GOD: ALWAYS ABOUNDING IN THE WORK OF THE LORD

Wherefore, my beloved brethren, be ye stedfast, unmoveable, always abounding in the work of the Lord, forasmuch as ye know that your labour is not in vain in the Lord.

1 CORINTHIANS 15:58

*W*E all know the fifteenth chapter of 1st Corinthians, in its Divine revelation of the meaning of Christ's resurrection, with all the blessings of which it is the source.

It gives us a living Saviour, who revealed Himself to His disciples on earth, and to Paul from heaven. It secures to us the complete deliverance from all sin. It is the pledge of His final victory over every enemy, when He gives up the kingdom to the Father, and God is all in all. It assures us of the resurrection of the body, and our entrance on the heavenly life. Paul had closed his argument with his triumphant appeal to Death and Sin and the Law: "O Death, where is thy victory? The sting of Death is Sin, and the power of Sin is the Law. But thanks be to God, which giveth us the victory through our Lord Jesus Christ."[72] And then follows, after fifty-seven verses of exultant teaching

72 "O Death...": 1 Corinthians 15:55-57.

concerning the mystery and the glory of the resurrection life in our Lord and His people, just one verse of practical application: "Wherefore, my beloved brethren, be ye stedfast, unmoveable, always abounding in the work of the Lord." The faith in a risen, living Christ, and in all that His resurrection is to us in time and eternity, is to fit us for, is to prove itself in—abounding[73] work for our Lord!

It cannot be otherwise. Christ's resurrection was His final victory over sin, and death, and Satan, and His entrance upon His work of giving the Spirit from heaven and extending His kingdom throughout the earth. Those who shared the resurrection joy at once received the commission to make known the joyful news. It was so with Mary and the women.[74] It was so with the disciples the evening of the resurrection day. "As the Father sent Me, I send you."[75] It was so with all to whom the charge was given: "Go into all the world, preach the Gospel to every creature."[76] The resurrection is the beginning and the pledge of Christ's victory over all the earth. That victory is to be carried out to its complete manifestation through His people. The faith and joy of the resurrection life are the inspiration and the power for the work of doing it. And so the call comes to all believers without exception: "Wherefore, my beloved brethren, be ye always abounding in the work of the Lord!"

"In the work of the Lord." The connection tells us at once what that work is. Nothing else, nothing less than, telling others of the risen Lord, and proving to them what new life Christ has brought to us. As we indeed know and acknowledge Him as Lord over all we are, and live in the

73 **Abounding:** A plentiful supply or perpetually producing.

74 "Mary and the women": A reference to Mary Magdalene and company at Christ's tomb (Matthew 28).

75 "As the Father...": John 20:21.

76 "Go into...": Mark 15:16.

joy of His service, we shall see that the work of the Lord is but one work—that of winning men to know and bow to Him. Amid all the forms of lowly, living, patient service, this will be the one aim, in the power of the life of the risen Lord, to make Him Lord of all.

This work of the Lord is no easy one. It cost Christ His life to conquer sin and Satan and gain the risen life. It will cost us our life, too—the sacrifice of the life of nature.[77] It needs the surrender of all on earth to live in the full power of resurrection newness of life. The power of sin, and the world, in those around us is strong, and Satan does not yield his servants an easy prey to our efforts. It needs a heart in close touch with the risen Lord, truly living the resurrection life, to be stedfast, unmoveable, always abounding in the work of the Lord. But that is a life that can be lived—because Jesus lives.

Paul adds: "Forasmuch as ye know that your labour is not vain in the Lord." I have spoken more than once of the mighty influence that the certainty of reward for work, in the shape of wages or riches, exerts on the millions of earth's workers. And shall not Christ's workers believe that, with such a Lord, their reward is sure and great? The work is often difficult and slow, and apparently fruitless. We are apt to lose heart, because we are working in our strength and judging by our expectations. Let us listen to the message: O ye children of the resurrection life, "be ye always abounding in the work of the Lord, forasmuch as ye know your labour is not in vain in the Lord." "Let not your hands be weak; your work shall be rewarded."[78] "You know that your labour is not vain in the Lord."

77   **Life of nature:** Here used to indicate our natural tendencies to do as we wish when we wish, to live our self-centered lives.

78   "Let not your hands be weak...": 2 Chronicles 15:7.

"In the Lord." The expression is a significant one. Study it in Romans 16, where it occurs ten times, where Paul uses the expressions: "Receive here in the Lord;" "my fellow-worker in Christ Jesus;" "who are in Christ, in the Lord;" "beloved in the Lord;" "approved in Christ;" "who labour in the Lord;" "chosen in the Lord." The whole life and fellowship and service of these saints had the one mark—they were, their labours were, in the Lord. Here is the secret of effectual[79] service. Your labour is not in vain in the Lord." As a sense of His presence and the power of His life is maintained, as all works are wrought in Him, His strength works in our weakness; our labour cannot be in vain in the Lord. Christ said: "He that abideth in Me, and I in him, the same bringeth forth much fruit."[80] Oh! let not the children of this world, with their confidence that the masters whose work they are doing will certainly give them their due reward, put the children of light to shame. Let us rejoice and labour in the confident faith of the word: "Your labour is not in vain in the Lord. Wherefore, beloved brethren, be ye always abounding in the work of the Lord."

79 **Effectual:** Successful in producing the desired result.

80 "He that abideth...": John 15:5.

WORKING FOR GOD: ABOUNDING GRACE FOR ABOUNDING WORK

And God is able to make all grace abound unto you, that ye may abound unto every good work.
2 CORINTHIANS 9:8

*I*N our previous meditation we had the great motive to abounding work—the spirit of triumphant joy which Christ's resurrection inspires as it covers the past and the future. Our text to-day assures us that for this abounding work we have the ability provided: God is able to make all grace abound, that we may abound to all good works. Every thought of abounding grace is to be connected with the abounding in good works for which it is given. And every thought of abounding work is to be connected with the abounding grace that fits for it.

Abounding grace has abounding work for its aim. It is often thought that grace and good works are at variance with each other. This is not so. What Scripture calls the works of the law, our own works, the works of righteousness which we have done, dead works—works by which we seek to merit or to be made fit for God's favour, these are indeed the very opposite of grace. But they are also the very opposite of the good works which spring from grace, and for which alone grace is bestowed. As irreconcilable as are the works of the law with the freedom of grace, so essential and indispensable are the works of faith, good works, to the true Christian life. God makes grace to abound, that good works may abound. The measure of true grace is tested and proved by the measure of good works. God's grace abounds in us that we may abound in good works. We need to have the truth deeply rooted in us: Abounding grace has abounding work for its aim.

And abounding work needs abounding grace as its source and strength. There often is abounding work without abounding grace. Just as any man may be very diligent in an earthly pursuit, or a heathen in his religious service of an idol, so men may be very diligent in doing religious work in their own strength, with but little thought of that grace which alone can do true, spiritual effective work. For all work that is to be really acceptable to God, and truly fruitful, not only for some visible result here on earth, but for eternity, the grace of God is indispensable. Paul continually speaks of his own work as owing everything to the grace of God working in him: "I laboured more abundantly than they all: yet not I, but the grace of God which was with me" (1 Cor. 15:10). "According to the gift of that grace of God which was given me according to the working of His power" (Eph. 3:7). And he as frequently calls upon Christians to exercise their gifts "according to the grace that was given us" (Rom. 12:6). "The grace given according to the measure of the gift of Christ" (Eph. 4:7). It is only by the grace of God working in us that we can do what are truly good works. It is only as we seek and receive abounding grace that we can abound in every good work.

God is able to make all grace abound unto you, that ye may abound in all good works." With what thanksgiving every Christian ought to praise God for the abounding grace that is thus provided for him. And with what humiliation to confess that the experience of, and the surrender to, that abounding grace has been so defective. And with what confidence to believe that a life abounding in good works is indeed possible, because the abounding grace for it is so sure and so Divinely sufficient.

And then, with what simple childlike dependence to wait upon God day by day to receive the more grace which He gives to the humble.

Child of God! do take time to study and truly apprehend God's purpose with you, that you abound in every good work! He means it! He has provided for it! Make the measure of your consecration[81] to Him nothing less than His purpose for you. And claim, then, nothing less than the abounding grace He is able to bestow. Make His omnipotence[82] and His faithfulness your confidence. And live ever in the practice of continual prayer and dependence upon His power working in you. This will make you abound in every good work. According to your faith be it unto you.

Christian worker, learn here the secret of all failure and all success. Work in our own strength, with little

81   **Consecration:** Setting aside or declaring something sacred.

82   **Omnipotence:** Having unlimited or very great power.

prayer and waiting on God for His spirit, is the cause of failure. The cultivation of the spirit of absolute impotence and unceasing dependence will open the heart for the workings of the abounding grace. We shall learn to ascribe all we do to God's grace. We shall learn to measure all we have to do by God's grace. And our life will increasingly be in the joy of God's making His grace to abound in us, and our abounding in every good work.

1. "That ye may abound to every good work." Pray over this now till you feel that this is what God has prepared for you.

2. If your ignorance and feebleness appear to make it impossible, present yourself to God, and say you are willing, if He will enable you to abound in good works, to be a branch that brings forth much fruit.

3. Take into your heart, as a living seed, the precious truth: God is able to make all grace abound in you. Trust His power and His faithfulness (Rom. 4:20, 21; 1 Thess. 5:24).

4. Begin at once by doing lowly deeds of love. As the little child in the kindergarten. Learn by doing.

FIFTEENTH DAY

WORKING FOR GOD: IN THE WORK OF MINISTERING

And he gave some to be apostles; and some, prophets; and some, evangelists; and some, pastors and teachers; for the perfecting of the saints, unto the work of ministering, unto the building up of the body of Christ.

EPHESIANS 4:11, 12

83 **Bestowed:** To give or present.

*T*HE object with which Christ when He ascended to heaven bestowed[83] on His servants the various gifts that are mentioned is threefold. Their first aim is—for the perfecting of the saints. Believers as saints are to be led on in the pursuit of holiness until they stand perfect and complete in all the will of God." It was for this Epaphras laboured in prayer. It is of this Paul writes: "Whom we preach, teaching every man in all wisdom that we may present every man perfect in Christ" (Col. 4:12; 1:28).

This perfecting of the saints is, however, only a means to a higher end: unto the work of ministering, to fit all the saints to take their part in the service to which every believer is called. It is the same word as is used in texts as these: "They ministered to Him of their substance;" "Ye ministered to the saints and do minister" (Luke 4:30, 8:3; 1 Cor. 16:15; Heb. 6:10; 1 Pet. 4:11).

And this, again, is also a means to a still higher end: unto the building up of the body of Christ. As every member of our body takes its part in working for the health and growth and maintenance of the whole, so every member of the body of Christ is to consider it his first great duty to take part in all that can help to build up the body of Christ. And this, whether by the helping and strengthening of those who are already members, or the ingathering of those who are to belong to It. And the great work of the Church is, through its pastors and teachers, so to labour for the perfecting of the saints in holiness and love and fitness for service, that every one may take his part in the work of ministering, that so, the body of Christ may be built up and perfected.

Of the three great objects with which Christ has given His Church apostles and teachers, the work of ministering stands thus in the middle. On the one hand, it is preceded by that on which it absolutely depends—the perfecting of the saints. On the other, it is followed by that which it is meant to accomplish—the building up of the body of Christ. Every believer without exception, every member of Christ's body, is called to take part in the work of ministering. Let every reader try and realise the sacredness of his holy calling.

Let us learn what the qualification is for our work. "The perfecting of the saints" prepares them for the "work of ministering." It is the lack of true sainthood, of true holiness, that causes such lack and feebleness of service. As Christ's saints are taught and truly learn what conformity to Christ means, a life like his, given up in self-sacrifice for the service and salvation of men, as His humility and love, His separation from the world and devotion to the fallen, are seen to be the very essence and blessedness of the life He gives, the work of ministering, the ministry of love, will become the one thing we live for. Humility and Love—these are the two great virtues of the saint—they are the two great powers for the work of ministering. Humility makes us willing to serve; love makes us wise to know how to do it. Love is inventive; it seeks patiently, and suffers long, until it find a way to reach its object. Humility and love are equally turned away from self and its claims. Let us pray, let the Church labour for "the perfecting of the saints" in humility and love, and the Holy Spirit will teach us how to minister.

Let us look at what the great work is the members of Christ have to do. It is to minister to each other. Place yourself at Christ's disposal for service to your fellow Christians. Count yourself their servant. Study their interest. Set yourself actively to promote the welfare of the Christians round you. Selfishness may hesitate, the feeling of feebleness may discourage, sloth[84] and ease may raise difficulties—ask your Lord to reveal to you His will, and give yourself up to it. Round about you there are Christians who are cold and worldly and wandering from their Lord. Begin to think what you can do for them. Accept as the will of the Head[85] that you as a member should care for them. Pray for the Spirit of love. Begin

84   **Sloth:** Laziness.

85   **Head:** A reference to Christ.

somewhere—only begin, and do not continue hearing and thinking while you do nothing. Begin the work of "ministering" according to the measure of the grace you have. He will give more grace.

Let us believe in the power that worketh in us as sufficient for all we have to do. As I think of the thumb and finger holding the pen with which I write this, I ask, How is it that during all these seventy years of my life they have always known just to do my will? It was because the life of the head passed into and worked itself out in them. "He that believeth on Me," as his Head working in him, "the works that I do shall he do also."[86] Faith in Christ, whose strength is made perfect in our weakness, will give the power for all we are called to do.

Let us cry to God that all believers may waken up to the power of this great truth: Every member of the body is to live wholly for the building up of the body.

1. To be a true worker the first thing is close, humble fellowship with Christ the Head, to be guided and empowered by Him.

2. The next is humble, loving fellowship with Christ's members serving one another in love.

3. This prepares and fits for service in the world.

86   "He that believeth…": John 14:12.

WORKING FOR GOD: ACCORDING TO THE WORKING OF EACH SEVERAL PART

That we may grow up in all things into Him,
which is the Head, even Christ; from whom all
the body fitly framed and knit together through
that which every joint together supplieth,
according to the working in due measure of
each several part, maketh the increase of the
body unto the building up of itself in love.
EPHESIANS 4:15, 16

THE Apostle is here speaking of the growth, the increase, the building up of the body. This growth and increase has, as we have seen, a double reference. It includes both the spiritual uniting and strengthening of those who are already members, so as to secure the health of the whole body; and also the increase of the body by the addition of all who are as yet outside of it, and are to be gathered in. Of the former we spoke in the previous chapter—the mutual interdependence of all believers, and the calling to care for each other's welfare. In this chapter we look at the growth from the other side—the calling of every member of Christ's body to labour for its increase by the labour of love that seeks to bring in them who are not yet of it. This increase of the body and building up of itself in love can only be by the working in due measure of each several part.

Think of the body of a child; how does it reach the stature of a full-grown man? In no other way but by the working in due measure of every part. As each member takes its part, by the work it does in seeking and taking and assimilating[87] food, the increase is made by its building up itself. Not from without, but from within, comes the work that assures the growth. In no other way can Christ's body attain to the stature of the fulness of Christ. As it is unto Christ the Head we grow up, and from Christ the Head that the body maketh increase of itself, so it is all through that which every joint supplieth, according to the working in due measure of each several part. Let us see what this implies.

The body of Christ is to consist of all who believe in Him throughout the world. There is no possible way in which these members of the body can be gathered in, but by the body building itself up in love. Our Lord has made Himself, as Head, absolutely dependent on His members to do this work. What nature teaches us of our own bodies, Scripture teaches us of Christ's body. The head of a child may have thought and plans of growth—they will all be vain, except as the members all do their part in securing that growth. Christ Jesus has committed to His Church the growth and increase of His body. He asks and expects that as wholly as He the Head lives for the growth

87   **Assimilating:** Being absorbed and integrated, here referencing the digesting of food.

and welfare of the body, every member of His body, the very feeblest, shall do the same, to the building up of the body in love. Every believer is to count it his one duty and blessedness to live and labour for the increase of the body, the ingathering of all who, are to be its members.

What is it that is needed to bring the Church to accept this calling, and to train and help the members of the body to know and fulfil it? One thing. We must see that the new birth and faith, that all insight into truth, with all resolve and surrender and effort to live according to it, is only a preparation for our true work. What is needed is that in every believer Jesus Christ be so formed, so dwell in the heart, that His life in us shall be the impulse and inspiration of our love to the whole body, and our life for it. It is because self occupies the heart that it is so easy and natural and pleasing to care for ourselves. When Jesus Christ lives in us, it will be as easy and natural and pleasing to live wholly for the body of Christ. As readily and naturally as the thumb and fingers respond to the will and movement of the head will the members of Christ's body respond to the Head, as the body grows up into Him, and from Him maketh increase of itself.

Let us sum up. For the great work the Head is doing in gathering in from throughout the world and building up His body, He is entirely dependent on the service of the members. Not only our Lord, but a perishing world is waiting and calling for the Church to awake and give herself wholly to this work—the perfecting of the number of Christ's members. Every believer, the very feeblest, must learn to know his calling—to live with this as the main object of this existence. This great truth will be revealed to us in power, and obtain the mastery, as we give ourselves to the work of ministering according to the grace we already have. We may confidently wait for the full revelation of Christ in its as the power to do all He asks of us.

SEVENTEENTH DAY

WORKING FOR GOD: WOMEN ADORNED WITH GOOD WORK

Let women adorn themselves; not with braided hair, and gold or pearls or costly raiment; but through good works. Let none be enrolled as a widow under threescore years old, well reported of for good works; . . . if she hath diligently followed every good work.

1 TIMOTHY 2:10, 5:9, 10

88 **Pastoral Epistles:** 1 Timothy, 2 Timothy, and Titus.

89 **Ensample:** An example of something, in this case, good works.

*I*N the three Pastoral Epistles,[88] written to two young pastors to instruct them in regard to their duties, "good works" are more frequently mentioned than in Paul's other Epistles. In writing to the Churches, as in a chapter like Romans 12 he mentions the individual good work by name. In writing to the pastors he had to use this expression as a summary of what, both in their own life and their teaching of others, they had to aim at. A minister was to be prepared to every good work, furnished completely to every good work, an ensample[89] of good works. And they were to teach Christians—the women to adorn themselves with good works, diligently to follow every good work, to be well reported of for good works;

the men to be rich in good works, zealous of good works, ready to every good work, to be careful and to learn to maintain good works. No portion of God's work presses home more definitely the absolute necessity of good works as an essential, vital element in the Christian life.

Our two texts speak of the good works of Christian women. In the first they are taught that their adorning is to be not with braided hair, and gold or pearls or costly raiment,[90] but, as becomes women preferring godliness, with good works. We know what adornment is. A leafless tree in winter has life; when spring comes it puts on its beautiful garments, and rejoices in the adornment of foliage and blossom. The adorning of Christian women is not to be in hair or pearls or raiment, but in good works. Whether it be the good works that have reference to personal duty and conduct, or those works of beneficence that aim at the pleasing and helping of our neighbor or those that more definitely seek the salvation of souls— the adorning that pleases God, that gives true heavenly beauty, that will truly attract others to come and serve God, too, is what Christian women ought to seek after. John saw the holy city descend from heaven, made ready as a bride adorned for her husband." The fine linen is the "righteous acts of the saints" (Rev. 21:2, 24:8). Oh! that every Christian woman might seek so to adorn herself as to please the Lord that loved her.

In the second passage we read of widows who were placed upon a roll of honour in the early Church, and to whom a certain charge was given over the younger women. No one was to be enrolled who was not well reported of

90   **Raiment:** Clothing.

for good works." Some of these are mentioned: if she has been known for the careful bringing up of her children, for her hospitality to strangers, for her washing the saints' feet, for her relieving the afflicted; and then there is added, if she hath diligently followed every good work." If in her home and out of it, in caring for her own children, for strangers, for saints, for the afflicted, her life has been devoted to good works, she may indeed be counted fit to be an example and guide to others. The standard is a high one. It shows us the place good works took in the early Church. It shows how woman's blessed ministry of love was counted on and encouraged. It shows how, in the development of the Christian life, nothing so fits for rule and influence as a life given to good works.

91 **Part and parcel:** An essential or integral element.

Good works are part and parcel[91] of the Christian life, equally indispensable to the health and growth of the individual, and to the welfare and extension of the Church. And yet what multitudes of Christian women there are whose active share in the good work of blessing their fellow-creatures is little more than playing at good works. They are waiting for the preaching of a full gospel, which shall encourage and help and compel them to give their lives so to work for their Lord, that they, too, may be well reported of as diligently following every good work. The time and money, the thought and heart given to jewels or costly raiment will be redeemed to its true object. Religion will no longer be a selfish desire for personal safety, but the joy of being like Christ, the helper and saviour of the needy. Work for Christ will take its true place as indeed the highest form of existence, the true adornment of the

Christian life. And as diligence in the pursuits of earth is honoured as one of the true elements of character and worth, diligently to follow good works in Christ's service will be found to give access to the highest reward and the fullest joy of the Lord.

1. We are beginning to awaken to the wonderful place woman can take in church and school and mission. This truth needs to be brought home to every one of the King's daughters, that the adorning in which they are to attract the world, to please their Lord, and enter His presence is—good works.

2. Woman, as the image of the weakness of God, "the meekness and gentleness of Christ,"[92] is to teach man the beauty and the power of the long-suffering, self-sacrificing ministry of love.

3. The training for the service of love begins in the home life; is strengthened in the inner chamber; reaches out to the needy around, and finds its full scope in the world for which Christ died.

[92] "The meekness and gentleness...": 2 Corinthians 10:1.

WORKING FOR GOD:
RICH IN GOOD WORKS

Charge them that are rich in the present world, that they do good, that they be rich in good works, that they be ready to distribute, willing to communicate, laying up for themselves a good foundation against the time to come, that they may lay hold on the life which is life indeed.

1 TIMOTHY 6:18

*I*F women are to regard good work as their adornment, men are to count them their riches. As good works satisfy woman's eye and taste for beauty, they meet man's craving for possession and power. In the present world riches have a wonderful significance. They are often God's reward on diligence, industry, and enterprise. They represent and embody the life-power that has been spent in procuring them. As such they exercise power in the honour or service they secure from others. Their danger consists in their being of this world, in their drawing off the heart from the living God and the heavenly treasures. They may become a man's deadliest enemy: How hardly shall they that have riches enter the kingdom of heaven!

The gospel never takes away anything from us without giving us something better in its stead. It meets the desire for riches by the command to be rich in good works. Good works are the coin that is current in God's kingdom: according to these will be the reward in the world to come. By abounding in good works we lay up for ourselves treasures in heaven. Even here on earth they constitute a treasure, in the testimony of a good conscience, in the consciousness of being well-pleasing to God (1 John 3) in the power of blessing others.

There is more. Wealth of gold is not only a symbol of the heavenly riches, it is actually, though so opposite in its nature, a means to it. Charge the rich that they do good, that they be ready to distribute, willing to communicate, laying up for themselves a good foundation. "Make to yourselves friends by means of the mammon of unrighteousness, that, when it fails, they may receive you into the eternal tabernacles."[93] Even as the widow's mite, the gifts of the rich, when given in the same spirit, may be an offering with which God is well pleased (Heb. 13:16). The man who is rich in money may become rich in good works, if he follows out the instructions Scripture lays down. The money must not be given to be seen of men but as unto the Lord. Nor as from an owner, but a steward[94] who administers the Lord's money, with prayer for His guidance. Nor with any confidence in its power or influence, but in deep dependence on Him who alone can make it a blessing. Nor as a substitute for, or bringing out from that personal work and witness, which each believer is to give. As all Christian work, so our money-giving has

[93] "Make to yourselves...": Luke 16:9.

[94] **Steward:** A person who manages resources for another person.

its value alone from the spirit in which it is done, even the spirit of Christ Jesus.

What a field there is in the world for accumulating these riches, these heavenly treasures. In relieving the poor, in educating the neglected, in helping the lost, in bringing the gospel to Christians and heathen in darkness, what investment might be made if Christians sought to be rich in good works, rich toward God. We may well ask the question, What can be done to waken among believers a desire for these true riches? Men have made a science of the wealth of nations, and carefully studied all the laws by which its increase and universal distribution can be promoted. How can the charge to be rich in good works find a response in the hearts that its pursuit shall be as much a pleasure and a passion as the desire for the riches of the present world?

All depends upon the nature, the spirit, there is in man. To the earthly nature, earthly riches have a natural affinity and irresistible attraction. To foster the desire for the acquisition of what constitutes wealth in the heavenly kingdom, we must appeal to the spiritual nature. That spiritual nature needs to be taught and educated and trained into all the business habits that go to make a man rich. There must be the ambition to rise above the level of a bare existence, the deadly contentment with just being saved. There must be some insight into the beauty and worth of good works as the expression of the Divine life—God's working in us and our working in Him; as the means of bringing glory to God; as the source of life and blessing to men; as the laying up of a treasure in heaven for eternity. There must be a faith that these riches are actually within our reach, because the grace and Spirit of God are working in us. And then the outlook for every opportunity of doing the work of God to those around us, in the footsteps of Him who said, "It is more blessed to give than receive."[95] Study and apply these principles— they will open the sure road to your becoming a rich man. A man who wants to be rich often begins on a small scale, but never loses an opportunity. Begin at once with some work of love, and ask Christ, who became poor, that you might be rich, to help you.

95   "It is more blessed...": Paul quotes these words of Jesus in Acts 20:35.

1.   What is the cause that the appeal for money for missions meets with such insufficient response? It is because of the low spiritual state of the Church. Christians have no due conception of their calling to live wholly for God and His kingdom.

2.   How can the evil be remedied? Only when believers see and accept their Divine calling to make God's kingdom their first care, and with humble confession of their sins yield themselves to God, will they truly seek the heavenly riches to be found in working for God.

3.   Let us never cease to plead and labour for a true spiritual awakening throughout the Church.

WORKING FOR GOD:
PREPARED UNTO EVERY
GOOD WORK

If a man therefore cleanse himself from them,
he shall be a vessel unto honour,
sanctified, meet for the Master's use,
prepared unto every good work.

2 TIMOTHY 2:21

*P*AUL had spoken of the foundation of God standing
sure (2:19), of the Church as the great house built
upon that foundation, of vessels, not only of gold, silver,
costly and lasting, vessels to honour, but also of wood and
of earth, common and perishable, vessels to dishonour.
He distinguishes between them of whom he had spoken,
who gave themselves to striving about words and to vain
babblings, and such as truly sought to depart from all
iniquity. In our text he gives us the four steps in the path
in which a man can become a vessel unto honour in the
great household of God. These are, the cleansing from sin;
the being sanctified; the meetness[96] for the Master to use
as He will; and last, the spirit of preparedness for every
good work. It is not enough that we desire or attempt to
do good works. As we need training and care to prepare us

96   **Meetness:** In this case,
readiness and availability.

for every work we are to do on earth, we need it no less, or rather we need it much more, to be—what constitutes the chief mark of the vessels unto honour—to be prepared unto every good work.

If a man "cleanse himself from them"—from that which characterises the vessels of dishonour—the empty profession leading to ungodliness, against which he had warned. In every dish and cup we use, how we insist upon it that it shall be clean. In God's house the vessels must much more be clean. And every one who would be truly prepared unto every good work must see to this first of all, that he cleanse himself from all that is sin. Christ Himself could not enter upon His saving work in heaven until He had accomplished the cleansing of our sins. How can we become partners in His work, unless there be with us the same cleansing first. Ere Isaiah could say, "Here am I, send me,"[97] the fire of heaven had touched his lips, and he heard the voice, "Thy sin is purged."[98] An intense desire to be cleansed from every sin lies at the root of fitness for true service.

"He shall be a vessel of honour, sanctified." Cleansing is the negative side, the emptying out and removal of all that is impure. Sanctified, the positive side, the refilling and being possessed of the spirit of holiness, through whom the soul becomes God-possessed, and so partakes of His holiness. "Let us cleanse ourselves from all defilement of flesh and spirit"—this first, then, and so "perfecting holiness in the fear of the Lord."[99] In the temple the vessels were not only to be clean, but holy, devoted to God's service alone. He that would truly work

97   "Here am I...": Isaiah 6:8.

98   "Thy sin...": Isaiah 6:7.

99   "Let us cleanse..." and "so perfecting...": 2 Corinthians 7:1.

for God must follow after holiness; "a heart established in holiness" (1 Thess. 4:14), a holy habit of mind and disposition, yielded up to God and marked by a sense of His presence, fit for God's work. The cleansing from sin secures the filling with the Spirit.

"Meet for the Master's use." We are vessels for our Lord to use. In every work we do, it is to be Christ using us and working through us. The sense of being a servant, dependent on the Master's guidance, working under the Master's eye, instruments used by Him and His mighty power, lies at the root of effectual service. It maintains that unbroken dependence, that quiet faith, through which the Lord can do His work. It keeps up that blessed consciousness of the work being all His, which leads the worker to become the humbler the more be is used. His one desire is—meet for the Master's use.

"Prepared unto every good work." Prepared. The word not only means equipment, fitness, but also the disposition, the alacrity which keeps a man on the outlook, and makes him earnestly desire and joyfully avail himself of every opportunity of doing his Master's work. As he lives in touch with his Lord Jesus, and holds himself as a cleansed and sanctified vessel, ready for Him to use, and he sees how good works are what he was redeemed for, and what his fellowship with his Lord is to be proved in, they become the one thing he is to live for. He is prepared unto every good work.

1. Meet for the Master's use," that is the central thought. A personal relation to Christ, an entire surrender to His disposal, a dependent

waiting to be used by Him, a joyful confidence that He will use us—such is the secret of true work.

2.   Let the beginning of your work be a giving yourself into the hands of the Master, as your living, loving Lord.

WORKING FOR GOD: FURNISHED COMPLETELY UNTO EVERY GOOD WORK

Give diligence to present thyself approved unto God, a workman that needeth not to be ashamed, handling aright the word of truth.

2 TIMOTHY 2:15

Every scripture inspired of God is also profitable for teaching, for reproof, for correction, for instruction which is in righteousness; that the man of God may be complete, furnished completely unto every good work.

2 TIMOTHY 3:16, 17

"*A* workman that needeth not to be ashamed" is one who is not afraid to have the master come and inspect his work. In hearty devotion to it, in thoroughness and skill, he presents himself approved to him who employs him. God's workers are to give diligence to present themselves approved to Him; to have their work worthy of Him unto all well-pleasing. They are to be as a workman that needeth not to be ashamed. A workman is one who knows his work, who gives himself wholly to it, who is known as a working man, who takes delight in doing his work well. Such every Christian minister, every Christian worker, is to be—a workman that makes a study of it to invite and expect the Master's approval.

"Handling aright the word of truth." The word is a seed, a fire, a hammer, a sword, is bread, is light. Workmen in any of these spheres can be our example. In work for God everything depends upon handling the word aright. Therefore it is that, in the second text quoted above, the personal subjection[100] to the word, and the experience of its power, is spoken of as the one means of our being completely furnished to every good work. God's workers must know that the Scripture is inspired of God, and has the life and life-giving power of God in it. Inspired is Spirit-breathed—the life in a seed, God's Holy Spirit is in the word. The Spirit in the word and the Spirit in our heart is One. As by the power of the Spirit within us we take the Spirit-filled word we become spiritual men. This word is given for teaching, the revelation of the thoughts of God; for reproof,[101] the discovery of our sins and mistakes; for correction, the removal of what is defective to be replaced by what is right and good; for instruction which is in righteousness, the communication of all the knowledge needed to walk before God in His ways. As one yields himself wholly and heartily to all this, and the true Spirit-filled word gets mastery of his whole being, he becomes a man of God, complete and furnished completely to every good work. He becomes a workman approved of God, who needs not to be ashamed, rightly handling the word of God. And so the man of God has

100 **Subjection:** The state of being controlled by; in this case, a decision to put the Word of God in control of one's life.

101 **Reproof:** To surface and confront a fault.

the double mark—his own life wholly moulded by the Spirit-breathed word—and his whole work directed by his rightly handling that word.

"That the man of God may be complete, thoroughly furnished unto every good work." In our previous meditation we learnt how in the cleansing and sanctification of the personal life the worker becomes a vessel meet for the Masters use, prepared unto every good work. Here we learn the same lesson—it is the man of God who allows God's word to do its work of reproving and correcting and instructing in his own life who will be complete, completely furnished unto every good work. Complete equipment[102] and readiness for every good work—that is what every worker for God must aim at.

If any worker, conscious of how defective his preparation is, ask how this complete furnishing for every good work is to be attained, the analogy of an earthly workman, who needs not be ashamed, suggests the answer. He would tell us that he owes his success, first of all, to devotion to his work. He gave it his close attention. He left other things to concentrate his efforts on mastering one thing. He made it a life-study to do his work perfectly. They who would do Christ's work as a second thing, not as the first, and who are not willing to sacrifice all for it, will never be complete or completely furnished to every good work.

The second thing he will speak of will be patient training and exercise. Proficiency only comes through painstaking effort. You may feel as if you know not how or what to work aright. Fear not—all learning begins with

102 **Equipment:** In this use, to be equipped for a task or mission.

ignorance and mistakes. Be of good courage. He who has endowed human nature with the wonderful power that has filled the world with such skilled and cunning workmen, will He not much more give His children the grace they need to be His fellow-workers? Let the necessity that is laid upon you—the necessity that you should glorify God, that you should bless the world, that you should through work ennoble and perfect your life and blessedness, urge you to give immediate and continual diligence to be a workman completely furnished unto every good work.

It is only in doing we learn to do aright. Begin working under Christ's training; He will perfect His work in you, and so fit you for your work for him.

1. The work God is doing, and seeking to have done in the world, is to win it back to Himself.

2. In this work every believer is expected to take part.

3. God wants us to be skilled workmen, who give our whole heart to His work, and delight in it.

4. God does His work by working in us, inspiring and strengthening us to do His work.

5. What God asks is a heart and life devoted to Him in surrender and faith.

6. As God's work is all love, love is the power that works in us, inspiring our efforts and conquering its object.

WORKING FOR GOD: ZEALOUS OF GOOD WORKS

He gave Himself for us, that He might redeem
us from all iniquity, and purify us for Himself, a
people of His own, zealous of good works.

TITUS 2:14

*I*N these words we have two truths—what Christ has done to make ßus His own, and what He expects of us. In the former we have a rich and beautiful summary of Christ's work for us: He gave Himself for us, He redeemed us from all iniquity,[103] He cleansed us for Himself, He took us for a people, for His own possession. And all with the one object, that we should be a people zealous of good works. The doctrinal half of this wonderful passage has had much attention bestowed on it; let us devote our attention to its practical part—we are to be a people zealous of good works. Christ expects of us that we shall be zealots for good works—ardently,[104] enthusiastically devoted to their performance.

This cannot be said to be the feeling with which most Christians regard good works. What can be done to cultivate this disposition? One of the first things that wakens zeal in work is a great and urgent sense of need.

103 **Iniquity:** Sinful behavior.

104 **Ardently:** With enthusiasm or passion.

A great need wakens strong desire, stirs the heart and the will, rouses all the energies of our being. It was this sense of need that roused many to be zealous of the law; they hoped their works would save them. The Gospel has robbed this motive of its power. Has it taken away entirely the need of good works? No, indeed, it has given that urgent need a higher place than before. Christ needs, needs urgently, our good works. We are His servants, the members of His body, without whom He cannot possibly carry on His work on earth. The work is so great—with the hundreds of millions of the unsaved—the work is so great, that not one worker can be spared. There are thousands of Christians to-day who feel that their own business is urgent, and must be attended to, and have no conception of the urgency of Christ's work committed to them. The Church must waken up to teach each believer this.

As urgently as Christ needs our good works the world needs them. There are around you men and women and children who need saving. To see men swept down past us in a river, stirs our every power to try and save them. Christ has placed His people in a perishing world, with the expectation that they will give themselves, heart and soul, to carry on His work of love. Oh! let us sound forth the blessed Gospel message: He gave Himself for us that He might redeem us for Himself, a people of His own, to serve Him and carry on His work—zealous of good works.

A second great element of zeal in work is delight in it. An apprentice or a student mostly begins his work under a sense of duty. As he learns to understand and enjoy it, he does it with pleasure, and becomes zealous in its performance. The Church must train Christians to believe that when once we give our hearts to it, and seek for the training that makes us in some degree skilled workmen, there is no greater joy than that of sharing in Christ's work of mercy and beneficence. As physical and mental activity give pleasure, and call for the devotion and zeal of thousands, the spiritual service of Christ can waken our highest enthusiasm.

Then comes the highest motive, the personal one of attachment to Christ our Redeemer: "The love of Christ constraineth us."[105] The love of Christ to us is the source and measure of our love to Him. Our love to Him becomes the power and the measure of our love to souls. This love, shed abroad in our hearts by the Holy Spirit, this love as a Divine communication, renewed in us by the renewing of the Holy Ghost day by day, becomes a zeal for Christ that shows itself as a zeal for good works. It becomes the link that unites the two parts of our text, the doctrinal and the practical, into one. Christ's love, that gave Himself for us, that redeemed us from all iniquity, that cleansed us for Himself, that made us a people of His own in the bonds of an everlasting loving kindness, that love believed in, known, received into the heart, makes the redeemed soul of necessity zealous in good works.

"Zealous of good works!" Let no believer, the youngest, the feeblest, look upon this grace as too high. It is Divine, provided for and assured in the love of our Lord. Let us accept it as our calling. Let us be sure it is the very nature of the new life within us. Let us, in opposition to all that nature or feeling may say, in faith claim it as an integral part of our redemption—Christ Himself will make it true in us.

105 "The love of Christ constraineth us": 2 Corinthians 5:14.

WORKING FOR GOD:
READY TO EVERY
GOOD WORK

Put them in mind to be ready
to every good work.

TITUS 3:1

" *P*UT them in mind." The words suggest the need of believers to have the truths of their calling to good works ever again set before them. A healthy tree spontaneously bears its fruit. Even where the life of the believer is in perfect health, Scripture teaches us how its growth and fruitfulness only come through teaching, and the influence that exerts on mind and will and heart. For all who have charge of others the need is great of Divine wisdom and faithfulness to teach and train all Christians, specially young and feeble Christians, to be ready to every good work. Let us consider some of the chief points of such training.

Teach them clearly what good works are. Lay the foundation in the will of God, as revealed in the law, and show them how integrity and righteousness and obedience are the groundwork of Christian character. Teach them how in all the duties and relationships of daily life true religion is to be carried out. Lead them on to the virtues which Jesus specially came to exhibit and teach—humility, meekness and gentleness and love. Open out to them the meaning of a life of love, self-sacrifice, and beneficence[106]—entirely given to think of and care for others. And then carry them on to what is the highest, the true life of good works—the winning of men to know and love God.

Teach them what an essential part of the Christian life good works are. They are not, as many think, a secondary element in the salvation which God gives. They are not merely to be done in token of our gratitude, or as a proof of the sincerity of our faith, or as a preparation for heaven. They are all this, but they are a great deal more. They are the very object for which we have been redeemed: we have been created anew unto good works. They alone are the evidence that man has been restored to his original destiny of working as God Works, and with God, and because God works through him. God has no higher glory than His works, and specially His work of saving love. In becoming imitators of God, and walking and working in love, "even as Christ loved us and gave Himself for us,"[107] we have the very image and likeness of God restored in us. The works of a man not only reveal his life, they develop and exercise, they strengthen and perfect it. Good works are of the very essence of the Divine life in us.

Teach them, too, what a rich reward they bring. All labour has its market value. From the poor man who scarce can earn a shilling[108] a day, to the man who has made his millions, the thought of the reward there is for

106 **Beneficence:** Goodness and generosity.

107 "even as Christ...": Ephesians 5:2.

108 **Shilling:** At the time, a British coin equal to one twentieth of a pound; an unsubstantial amount of money.

labour has been one of the great incentives to undertake it. Christ appeals to this feeling when He says, "Great shall be your reward."[109] Let Christians understand that there is no service where the reward is so rich as that of God. Work is bracing, work is strength, and cultivates the sense of mastery and conquest. Work wakens enthusiasm and calls out a man's noblest qualities. In a life of good works the Christian becomes conscious of his Divine ministry of dispensing the life and grace of God to others. They bring us into closer union with God. There is no higher fellowship with God than fellowship in His saving work of love. It brings us into sympathy with Him and His purposes; it fills us with His love; it secures His approval. And great is the reward, too, on those around us. When others are won to Christ, when the weary and the erring and the desponding are helped and made partakers of the grace and life there are in Christ Jesus for them, God's servants share in the very joy in which our blessed Lord found His recompense.

And now the chief thing. Teach them to believe that it is possible for each of us to abound in good works. Nothing is so fatal to successful effort as discouragement or despondency. Nothing is more a frequent cause of neglect of good works than the fear that we have not the power to perform them. Put them in mind of the power of the Holy Spirit dwelling in them. Show them that God's promise and provision of strength is always equal to what He demands; that there is always grace sufficient for all the good works to which we are called. Strive to waken in them a faith in the power that worketh in us," and in the

109 "Great shall be...": Matthew 5:12.

fulness of that life which can flow out as rivers of living water. Train them to begin at once their service of love. Lead them to see how it is all God working in them, and to offer themselves as empty vessels to be filled with His love and grace. And teach them that as they are faithful in a little, even amid mistakes and shortcomings, the acting out of the life will strengthen the life itself, and work for God will become in full truth a second nature.

God grant that the teachers of the Church may be faithful to its commission in regard to all her members— Put them in mind to "be ready for every good work." Not only teach them, but train them. Show them the work there is to be done by them; see that they do it; encourage and help them to do it hopefully. There is no part of the office of a pastor more important or more sacred than this, or fraught with richer blessing. Let the aim be nothing less than to lead every believer to live entirely devoted to the work of God in winning men to Him. What a change it would make in the Church and the world!

1. Get a firm hold of the great root-principle. Every believer, every member of Christ's body, has his place in the body solely for the welfare of the whole body.

2. Pastors have been given for the perfecting of the saints with the work of ministering, of serving in love.

3. In ministers and members of the churches, Christ will work mightily if they will wait upon Him.

TWENTY-THIRD DAY

WORKING FOR GOD: CAREFUL TO MAINTAIN GOOD WORKS

I will that thou affirm these things confidently,
to the end that they which have believed God
may be careful to maintain good works. Let our
people also learn to maintain good works for
necessary uses, that they be not unfruitful.

TITUS 3:8, 14

*I*N the former of these passages Paul charges Titus confidently to affirm the truths of the blessed Gospel to the end, with the express object[110] that all who had believed should be careful, should make a study of it, to maintain good works. Faith and good works were to be inseparable; the diligence of every believer in good works was to be a main aim of a pastor's work. In the second passage he reiterates the instruction, with the expression, let them learn, suggesting the thought that, as all work on earth has to be learned, so in the good works of the Christian life there is an equal need of thought and application and teachableness, to learn how to do them aright and abundantly.

110 **Object:** In this case, the intended thing to which one's actions are directed.

111 **Conventionalities:**
Normal and accepted
rules of behavior.

There may be more than one reader of this little book who has felt how little he has lived in accordance with all the teaching of God's word, prepared, thoroughly furnished, ready unto, zealous of good works. It appears so difficult to get rid of old habits, to break through the conventionalities[111] of society, to know how to begin and really enter upon a life that can be full of good works, to the glory of God. Let me try and give some suggestions that may be helpful. They may also aid those who have the training of Christian workers, in showing in what way the teaching and learning of good works may best succeed. Come, young workers all, and listen.

1. A learner must begin by beginning to work at once. There is no way of learning an art like swimming or music, a new language or a trade, but by practice. Let neither the fear that you cannot do it, nor the hope that something will happen that will make it easier for you, keep you back. Learn to do good works, the works of love, by beginning to do them. However insignificant they appear, do them. A kind word, a little help to some one in trouble, an act of loving attention to a stranger or a poor man, the sacrifice of a seat or a place to some one who longs for it—practise these things. All plants we cultivate are small at first. Cherish the consciousness that, for Jesus' sake, you are seeking to do what would please Him. It is only in doing you can learn to do.

2. The learner must give his heart to the work, must take interest and pleasure in it. Delight in

work ensures success. Let the tens of thousands around you in the world who throw their whole soul into their daily business, teach you how to serve your blessed Master. Think sometimes of the honour and privilege of doing good works, of serving others in love. It is God's own work, to love and save and bless men. He works it in you and through you. It makes you share the spirit and likeness of Christ. It strengthens your Christian character. Without actions, intentions lower and condemn a man instead of raising him. Only as much as you act out, do you really live. Think of the Godlike blessedness of doing good, of communicating life, of making happy. Think of the exquisite joy of growing up into a life of beneficence, and being the blessing of all you meet. Set your heart upon being a vessel meet for the Master's use, ready to every good work.

3. Be of good courage, and fear not. The learner who says I cannot, will surely fail. There is a Divine power working in you. Study and believe what God's word says about it. Let the holy self-reliance of St. Paul, grounded on his reliance on Christ, be your example: "I can do all things in Christ which strengtheneth me."[112] Study and take home to yourself the wonderful promises about the power of the Holy Spirit, the abundance of grace, Christ's strength made perfect in weakness, and see how all this can

112 "I can do all things...":
Philippians 4:13.

only be made true to you in working. Cultivate the noble consciousness that as you have been created to good works by God, He Himself will fit you for them. And believe then that just as natural as it is to any workman to delight and succeed in his profession, it can be to the new nature in you to abound in every good work. Having this confidence, you need never faint.

4.   Above all, cling to your Lord Jesus as your Teacher and Master. He said: "Learn of Me, for I am meek and lowly of heart, and ye shall find rest to your souls."[113] Work as one who is a learner in His school, who is sure that none teaches like Him, and is therefore confident of success. Cling to Him, and let a sense of His presence and His power working in you make you meek and lowly, and yet bold and strong. He who came to do the Father's work on earth, and found it the path to the Father's glory, will teach you what it is to work for God.

To sum up again, for the sake of any who want to learn how to work, or how to work better:

1.   Yield yourself to Christ. Lay yourself on the altar, and say you wish to give yourself wholly to live for God's work.

2.   Believe quietly that Christ accepts and takes charge of you for His work, and will fit you for it.

113   "Learn of Me...": Matthew 11:29.

3. Pray much that God would open to you the great truth of His own working in you. Nothing else can give true strength.

4. Seek to cultivate a spirit of humble, patient, trustful dependence upon God. Live in loving fellowship with Christ, and obedience to Him. You can count upon His strength being made perfect in your weakness.

WORKING FOR GOD:
AS HIS FELLOW-WORKERS

We are God's fellow-workers:
ye are God's building.

1 CORINTHIANS 3:9

And working together with Him we intreat
that ye receive not the grace of God in vain.

2 CORINTHIANS 6:1

*W*E have listened to Paul's teaching on good works (chaps. IX.-XXII.);[114] let us turn now to his personal experience, and see if we can learn from him some of the secrets of effective service.

He speaks here of the Church as God's building, which, as the Great Architect, He is building up into a holy temple and dwelling for Himself. Of his own work, Paul speaks as of that of a master builder, to whom a part of the great building has been given in charge. He had laid a foundation in Corinth; to all who were working there he said: "Let each man take heed how he buildeth thereon."[115] "We are God's fellow-workers." The word is applicable not only to Paul, but to all God's servants who take part in His work; and because every believer has been

114   **IX-XXII:** Days 9 through 22.

115   "Let each man take heed...": 1 Corinthians 3:10.

called to give his life to God's service and to win others to His knowledge, every, even the feeblest, Christian needs to have the word brought to him and taken home: "We are God's fellow-workers." How much it suggests in regard to our working for God!

As to the work we have to do—The eternal God is building for Himself a temple; Christ Jesus, God's Son, is the foundation; believers are the living stones. The Holy Spirit is the mighty power of God through which believers are gathered out of the world made fit for their place in the temple, and built up into it. As living stones, believers are at the same time the living workmen, whom God uses to carry out His work. They are equally God's workmanship and God's fellow-workers. The work God is doing He does through them. The work they have to do is the very work God is doing. God's own work, in which He delights, on which His heart is set, is saving men and building them into His temple. This is the one work on which the heart of every one who would be a fellow-worker with God must be set. It is only as we know how great, how wonderful, this work of God is—giving life to dead souls, imparting His own life to them, and living in them—that we shall enter somewhat into the glory of our work, receiving the very life of God from Him, and passing it on to men.

As to the strength for the work—Paul says of his work as a mere master builder, that it was "according to the grace of God which was given me."[116] For Divine work nothing but Divine power suffices. The power by which God works must work in us. That power is His

116 "according to the grace..." 2 Corinthians 1:12.

Holy Spirit. Study the second chapter of this Epistle, and the third of the Second, and see how absolute was Paul's acknowledgment of his own impotence, and his dependence on the teaching and power of the Holy Spirit. As this great truth begins to live in the hearts of God's workers, that God's work can only be done by God's power in us, we shall feel that our first need every day is to have the presence of God's Spirit renewed within us. The power of the Holy Spirit is the power of love. God is love. All He works for the salvation of men is love; it is love alone that truly conquers and wins the heart. In all God's fellow-workers love is the power that reaches the hearts of men. Christ conquered and conquers still by the love of the cross. Let that mind be in you, O worker, which was in Christ Jesus, the spirit of a love that sacrifices itself to the death, of a humble, patient, gentle love, and you will be made meet to be God's fellow-worker.

As to the relation we are to hold to God—In executing the plans of some great building the master builder has but one care—to carry out to the minutest detail the thoughts of the architect who designed it. He acts in constant consultation with him, and is guided in all by his will; and his instructions to those under him have all reference to the one thing—the embodiment, in visible shape, of what the master mind has conceived. The one great characteristic of fellow-workers with God ought to be that of absolute surrender to His will, unceasing dependence on His teaching, exact obedience to His wishes. God has revealed His plan in His Word. He has told us that His Spirit alone can enable us to enter into

His plans, and fully master His purpose with the way he desires to have it carried out. The clearer our insight into the Divine glory of God's work of saving souls, into the utter insufficiency of our natural powers to do the work, into the provision, that has been made by which the Divine love can animate[117] us, and the Divine Spirit guide and strengthen us for its due performance, the more we shall feel that a childlike teachableness, a continual looking upward and waiting on God, is ever to be the chief mark of one who is His fellow-labourer. Out of the sense of humility, helplessness, and nothingness there will grow a holy confidence and courage that knows that our weakness need not hinder us, that Christ's strength is made perfect in weakness, that God Himself is working out His purpose through us. And of all the blessings of the Christian life, the most wonderful will be that we are allowed to be—God's fellow-workers!

117 **Animate:** In this usage, to inspire and bring to life.

1. God's fellow-worker! How easy to use the word, and even to apprehend some of the great truths it contains! How little we live in the power and the glory of what it actually involves!

2. Fellow-workers with God! Everything depends upon knowing, in His holiness and love, the God with whom we are associated as partners.

3. He who has chosen us, that in and through us He might do His great work, will fit us for His use.

4. Let our posture be adoring worship, deep dependence, great waiting, full obedience.

WORKING FOR GOD:
ACCORDING TO THE
WORKING OF HIS POWER

> Whom we preach, warning every man, and teaching every man, that we may present every man perfect in Christ Jesus; whereunto I also labour, striving according to His working, which worketh in me mightily.
>
> **COLOSSIANS 1:29**

> The mystery of Christ, whereof I was made a minister, according to the gift of that grace of God which was given me according to the working of His power.
>
> **EPHESIANS 3:7**

*I*N the words of Paul to the Philippians, which we have already considered (Chap. IX.),[118] in which he called upon them and encouraged them to work, because it was God who worked in them, we found one of the most pregnant and comprehensive statements of the great truth that it is only by God's working in us that we can do true work. In our texts for this chapter we have Paul's testimony as to his own experience. His whole ministry was to be according to the grace which was given him according to the working of God's power. And of his labour he says that it was a striving according to the power of Him who worked mightily in him.

We find here the same principle we found in our Lord—the Father doing the works in Him. Let every worker who reads this pause, and say—If the ever-blessed Son, if the Apostle Paul, could only do their work according to the working of His power who worked in them mightily, how much more do I need this working of God in me, to fit me for doing His work aright. This is one of the deepest spiritual truths of God's word; let us look to the Holy Spirit within us to give it such a hold of our inmost life, that it may become the deepest inspiration of all our work. I can only do true work as I yield myself to God to work in me.

We know the ground on which this truth rests, "There is none good but God";[119] "There is none holy but the Lord";[120] "Power belongeth unto God."[121] All goodness and holiness and power are only to be found in God, and where He gives them. And He can only give them in the creature, not as something He parts with, but by His own actual presence and dwelling and working. And so God can only work in His people in as far as He is allowed to have complete possession of the heart and life. As our will and life and love are yielded up in dependence and faith, and God is waited on to keep possession and to abide, even as Christ waited on Him, God can work in us.

This is true of all our spiritual life, but specially of our work for God. The work of saving souls is God's own work: none but He can do it. The gift of His Son is the

119 "There is none good but God": Matthew 19:17.

120 "There is none holy but the Lord": 1 Samuel 2:2.

121 "Power belongeth...": Psalm 62:11.

proof of how great and precious He counts the work, and how His heart is set upon it. His love never for one moment ceases working for the salvation of men. And when He calls His children to be partners in His work, He shares with them the joy and the glory of the work of saving and blessing men. He promises to work His work through them, inspiring and energising them by His power working in them. To him who can say with Paul: "I labour, striving according to His power who worketh in me mightily," his whole relation to God becomes the counterpart and the continuation of Christ's, a blessed, unceasing, momentary, and most absolute dependence on the Father for every word He spoke and every work He did.

Christ is our pattern. Christ's life is our law and works in us. Christ lived in Paul his life of dependence on God. Why should any of us hesitate to believe that the grace given to Paul of labouring and striving according to the "working of the power" will be given to us too. Let every worker learn to say—As the power that worked in Christ worked in Paul too, that power works no less in me. There is no possible way of working God's work aright, but by God working it in us.

How I wish that I could take every worker who reads this by the hand, and say—Come, my brother! let us quiet our minds, and hush every thought in God's presence, as I whisper in your ears the wonderful secret: God is working in you. All the work you have to do for Him, God will work in you. Take time and think it over. It is a deep spiritual truth which the mind cannot grasp nor the heart realise. Accept it as a Divine truth from heaven; believe that this word is a seed out of which can grow the very spiritual blessing of which it speaks. And in the faith of the Holy Spirit's making it live within you, say ever again: God worketh in me. All the work I have to work for Him, God will work in me.

The faith of this truth, and the desire to have it made true in you, will constrain you to live very humbly and closely with God. You will see how work for God must be the most spiritual thing in a spiritual life. And you will ever anew how in holy stillness: God is working; God will work in me; I will work for Him according to the power which worketh in me mightily.

1. The gift of the grace of God (Eph. 2:7, Eph. 3:7), the power that worketh in us (Eph. 3:20), the strengthening with might by the Spirit (Eph. 3:16) —the three expressions all contain the same thought of God's working all in us.

2. The Holy Spirit is the power of God. Seek to be filled with the Spirit, to have your whole life led by Him, and you will become fit for God's working mightily in you.

3. "Ye shall receive the power of the Holy Spirit coming on you."[122] Through the Spirit dwelling in us God can work in us mightily.

4. What holy fear, what humble watchfulness and dependence, what entire surrender and obedience become us if we believe in God's working in us.

122 "Ye shall receive...": Acts 1:8.

WORKING FOR GOD: LABOURING MORE ABUNDANTLY

By the grace of God I am what I am: and His grace which was bestowed on me was not in vain; but I laboured more abundantly than they all: yet not I, but the grace of God which was with me.

1 CORINTHIANS 15:10

And He hath said unto me, My grace is sufficient for thee: for My power is made perfect in weakness. . . . In nothing was I behind the chiefest of the apostles, though I am nothing.

2 CORINTHIANS 12:9, 11

*I*N both of these passages Paul speaks of how he had abounded in the work of the Lord. "In nothing was I behind the chiefest of the Apostles." "I laboured more abundantly, than they all." In both he tells how entirely it was all of God, who worked in Him, and not of himself. In the first he says: "Not I, but the grace of God which was with me." And then in the second, showing how this grace is Christ's strength working in us, while we are nothing, he tells us: He said unto me: "My grace is sufficient for thee: My power is made perfect in weakness." May God give us the Spirit of revelation, enlightened eyes of the heart," to see this wonderful vision, a man who knows himself to be nothing, glorying in his weakness, that the power of Christ may rest on him, and work through him, and who so labours more abundantly than all. What does this teach us as workers for God.

God's work can only be done in God's strength—It is only by God's power, that is, by God Himself working in us, that we can do effective work. Throughout this little book this truth has been frequently repeated. It is easy to accept of it; it is far from easy to see its full meaning, to give it the mastery over our whole being, to live it out. This will need stillness of soul, and meditation, strong faith and fervent prayer. As it is God alone who can work in us, it is equally God who alone can reveal Himself as the God who works in us. Wait on Him, and the truth that ever appears to be beyond thy reach will be opened up to thee, through the knowledge of who and what God is. When God reveals Himself as "God who worketh all in all,"[123] thou wilt learn to believe and work "according to the power of Him who worketh in thee mightily."[124]

God's strength can only work in weakness—It is only when we truly say, Not I! that we can fully say, but the grace of God with me. The man who said, In nothing behind the chiefest[125] of the Apostles! had first learnt to say, though I am nothing. He could say: "I take pleasure in weaknesses, for when I am weak then am I strong."[126] This is the true relation between the Creator and the creature,

123 "God who worketh all in all": 1 Corinthians 12:6.

124 A reference to Colossians 1:29.

125 **Chiefest**: The first or foremost, in this case, referring to Paul.

126 "I take pleasure in weaknesses...": 2 Corinthians 12:10.

between the Divine Father and His child, between God and His servant. Christian worker! learn the lesson of thine own weakness, as the indispensable condition of God's Power working in thee. Do believe that to take time and in God's presence to realise thy weakness and nothingness is the sure way to be clothed with God's strength. Accept every experience by which God teaches thee thy weakness as His grace preparing thee to receive His strength. Take pleasure in weaknesses!

God's strength comes in our fellowship with Christ and His service—Paul says: "I will glory in my weakness, that the strength of Christ may rest upon me." "I take pleasure in weaknesses for Christ's sake." And he tells how it was when be had besought the Lord that the messenger of Satan might depart from him, that He answered: "My grace is sufficient for thee."[127] Christ is the wisdom and the power of God." We do not receive the wisdom to know, or the power to do God's will as something that we can possess and use at discretion. It is in the personal attachment to Christ, in a life of continual communication with Him, that His power rests on us. It is in taking pleasure in weaknesses for Christ's sake that Christ's strength is known.

God's strength is given to faith, and the work that is done in faith—It needs a living faith to take pleasure in weaknesses, and in weakness to do our work, knowing that God is working in us. Without seeing or feeling anything, to go on in the confidence of a hidden power working in us—this is the highest exercise of a life of faith. To do God's own work in saving souls, in persevering prayer and

127 "I will glory..." and "My grace is sufficient...": 2 Corinthians 12:9.

labour; amid outwardly unfavourable circumstances and appearances still to labour more abundantly—this faith alone can do. Let us be strong in faith, giving glory to God. God will show Himself strong towards him whose heart is perfect with Him.

My brother! be willing to yield yourself to the very utmost to God, that His power may rest upon you, may work in you. Do let God work through you. Offer yourself to Him for His work as the one object of your life. Count upon His working all in you, to fit you for His service, to strengthen and bless you in it. Let the faith and love of your Lord Jesus, whose strength is going to be made perfect in your weakness, lead you to live even as He did, to do the Father's will and finish His work.

1. Let every minister seek the full personal experience of Christ's strength made perfect in His weakness: this alone will fit him to teach believers the secret of their strength.

2. Our Lord says: My grace, My strength." It is as, in close personal fellowship and love, we abide in Christ, and have Christ abiding in us, that His grace and strength can work.

3. It is a heart wholly given up to God, to His will and love, that will know his power working in our weakness.

TWENTY-SEVENTH DAY

WORKING FOR GOD:
A DOER THAT WORKETH
SHALL BE BLESSED IN DOING

*Be ye doers of the word, and not hearers only,
deluding your own selves. He that looketh
into the perfect law, the law of liberty, and so
continueth, being not a hearer that forgetteth,
but a doer that worketh, this man shall
be blessed in doing.*

JAMES 1:22, 25

*G*OD created us not to contemplate but to act. He created us in His own image, and in Him there is no Thought without simultaneous Action. True action is born of contemplation. True contemplation, as a means to an end, always begets action. If sin had not entered there had never been a separation between knowing and doing. In nothing is the power of sin more clearly seen than this, that even in the believer there is such a gap between intellect and conduct. It is possible to delight in hearing, to be diligent in increasing our knowledge of God's word, to admire and approve the truth, even to be willing to do it, and yet to fail entirely in the actual performance. Hence the warning of James, not to delude ourselves with being hearers and not doers. Hence his pronouncing the doer who worketh blessed in his doing.

Blessed in doing   The words are a summary of the teaching of our Lord Jesus at the close of the Sermon on the Mount: "He that doeth the will of My Father shall enter the kingdom of heaven."[128] "Every one that heareth My words, and doeth them, shall be likened unto a wise man."[129] To the woman who spoke of the blessedness of her who was his mother: "Yea rather, blessed are they that hear the word of God and keep it."[130] To the disciples in the last night: "If ye know these things, happy are ye if ye do them."[131] It is one of the greatest dangers in religion that we rest content with the pleasure and approval which a beautiful representation of a truth calls forth, without the immediate performance of what it demands. It is only when conviction has been translated into conduct that we have proof that the truth is mastering us.

A doer that worketh shall be blessed in doing—The doer is blessed. The doing is the victory that overcomes every obstacle it brings out and confirms the very image of God, the Great Worker; it removes every barrier to the enjoyment of all the blessing God has prepared. We are ever inclined to seek our blessedness in what God gives, in privilege and enjoyment. Christ placed it in what we do, because it is only in doing that we really prove and know and possess the life God has bestowed. When one said, "Blessed is he that shall eat bread in the kingdom of God,"[132] our Lord answered with the parable of the supper,[133] Blessed is he that forsakes all to come to the supper. The doer is blessed. As surely as it is only in

128 "He that doeth the will of...": Matthew 7:21.

129 "Every one that heareth...": Matthew 7:24-27.

130 "Yea rather, blessed are...": Luke 11:28.

131 "If ye know these things..." John 13:17.

132 "Blessed is he that shall eat bread...": Luke 14:15.

133 **The Parable of the Supper** (or the Great Supper or Great Banquet): Luke 14:15-24.

doing that the painter or musician, the man of science or commerce, the discoverer or the conqueror find their blessedness, so, and much more, is it only in keeping the commandments and in doing the will of God that the believer enters fully into the truth and blessedness of deliverance from sin and fellowship with God. Doing is the very essence of blessedness, the highest manifestation, and therefore the fullest enjoyment of the life of God.

A doer that worketh shall be blessed in doing—This was the blessedness of Abraham, of whom we read (Jas. 2:22): "Thou seest that faith wrought with his works, and by works was faith made perfect." He had no works without faith ; there was faith working with them and in them all. And he had no faith without works: through them his faith was exercised and strengthened and perfected. As his faith, so his blessedness was perfected in doing. It is in doing that the doer that worketh is blessed. The true insight into this, as a Divine revelation of the true nature of good works, in perfect harmony with all our experience in the world, will make us take every command, and every truth, and every opportunity to abound in good works as an integral part of the blessedness of the salvation Christ has brought us. Joy and work, work and joy, will become synonymous: we shall no longer be hearers but doers.

Let us put this truth into immediate practice. Let us live for others, to love and serve them. Let not the fact of our being unused to labours of love, or the sense of ignorance and unfitness, keep us back. Only begin. If you think you are not able to labour for souls, begin with the bodies. Only begin, and go on, and abound. Believe the word, "It is more blessed to give than to receive."[134] Pray for and depend on the promised grace. Give yourself to a ministry of love; in the very nature of things, in the example of Christ, in the promise of God you have the assurance: If you know these things, happy are ye if ye do them. Blessed is the doer!

134 "It is more blessed to give...": Acts 20:35.

WORKING FOR GOD: THE WORK OF SOUL-SAVING

My brethren, if any of you do err from the truth,
and one convert him, let him know that he
which converteth a sinner from the error of his
ways shall save a soul from death, and shall
cover a multitude of sins.

JAMES 5:19-20

*W*E sometimes hesitate to speak of men being converted and saved by men. Scripture here twice uses the expression of one man converting another, and once of his saving him. Let us not hesitate to accept it as part of our work, of our high prerogative as the sons of God, to convert and to save men. "For it is God who worketh in us."[135]

135 A reference to Philippians 2:13.

"Shall save a soul from death." Every workman studies the material in which he works: the carpenter the wood, the goldsmith the gold. "Our works are wrought in God."[136] In our good works we deal with souls. Even when we can at first do no more than reach and help their bodies, our aim is the soul. For these Christ came to die. For these God has appointed us to watch and labour. Let us study these. What care a huntsman or a fisherman

136 A reference to John 3:21.

takes to know the habits of the spoil[137] he seeks. Let us remember that it needs Divine wisdom and training and skill to become winners of souls. The only way to get that training and skill is to begin to work: Christ Himself will teach each one who waits on Him.

In that training the Church with its ministers has a part to take.. The daily experience of ordinary life and teaching prove how often there exist in a man unsuspected powers, which must be called out by training before they are known to be there. When a man thus becomes conscious and master of the power there is in himself he is, as it were, a new creature; the power and enjoyment of life is doubled. Every believer has bidden within himself the power of saving souls. The Kingdom of Heaven is within us as a seed, and every one of the gifts and graces of the spirit are each also a hidden seed. The highest aim of the ministry is to waken the consciousness of this hidden seed of power to save souls. A depressing sense of ignorance or impotence keeps many back. James writes: "Let him who converts another know that he has saved a soul from death." Every believer needs to be taught to know and use the wondrous blessed power with which he has been endowed. When God said to Abraham: "I will bless thee, then shall all the nations of the earth be blessed,"[138] He called him to a faith not only in the blessing that would come to him from above, but in the power of blessing he would be in the world. It is a wonderful moment in the life of a child of God when he sees that the second blessing is as sure as the first.

137 **Spoil:** In this usage, something valuable that's to be obtained through effort.

138 "I will bless thee...": Genesis 22:18.

"He shall save a soul." Our Lord bears the name of Jesus, Saviour. He is the embodiment of God's saving love. Saving souls is His own great work, is His work alone. As our faith in Him grows to know and receive all there is in Him, as He lives in us, and dwells in our heart and disposition, saving souls will become the great work to which our life will be given. We shall be the willing and intelligent instruments through whom He will do His mighty work.

"If any err, and one convert him he which converteth a sinner shall save a soul." The words suggest personal work. We chiefly think of large gatherings to whom the Gospel is preached; the thought here is of one who has erred and is sought after. We increasingly do our work through associations and organisations. "If one convert him, he saveth a soul;" it is the love and labour of some individual believer that has won the erring one back. It is this we need in the Church of Christ,—every believer who truly follows Jesus Christ looking out for those who are erring from the way, loving them, and labouring to help them back. Not one of us may say, "Am I my brother's keeper?"[139] We are in the world only and solely that as the members of Christ's body we may continue and carry out His saving work. As saving souls was and is His work, His joy, His glory, let it be ours, let it be mine, too. Let me give myself personally to watch over individuals, and seek to save them one by one.

"Know that he which converteth a sinner shall save a soul." "If ye know these things, happy are ye if you do them."[140] Let me translate these Scripture truths into

139 "Am I my brother's keeper?": Cain's reply to God (Genesis 4:9) when asked about his brother, Abel.

140 "If ye know these things...": John 13:17.

action; let me give these thoughts shape and substance in daily life; let me prove their power over me, and my faith in them, by work. Is there not more than one Christian around me wandering from the way, needing loving help and not unwilling to receive it? Are there not some whom I could take by the hand, and encourage to begin again? Are there not many who have never been in the right way, for some of whom Christ Jesus would use me, if I were truly at His disposal?

If I feel afraid—oh! let me believe that the love of God as a seed dwells within me, not only calling but enabling me actually to do the work. Let me yield myself to the Holy Spirit to fill my heart with that love, and fit me for its service. Jesus the Saviour lives to save; He dwells in me; He will do His saving work through me. "Know that he which converteth a sinner shall save a soul from death, and cover a multitude of sins."

1.   More love to souls, born out of fervent love to the Lord Jesus—is not this our great need?

2.   Let us pray for love, and begin to love, in the faith that as we exercise the little we have more will be given.

3.   Lord! open our eyes to see Thee doing Thy great work of saving men, and waiting to give Thy love and strength into the heart of every willing one. Make each one of Thy redeemed a soul-winner.

WORKING FOR GOD: PRAYING AND WORKING

If any man see his brother sinning a sin not
unto death, he shall ask, and God will give him
life for them that sin not unto death.

1 JOHN 5:16

"*L*ET us consider one another to provoke unto love and good works"[141] these words in Hebrews express what lies at the very root of a life of good works—the thoughtful loving care we have for each other, that not one may fall away. As it is in Galatians: "Even if a man be overtaken in a trespass, ye which are spiritual, restore such a one in the spirit of meekness."[142] Or as Jude writes, apparently of Christians who were in danger of falling away, "Some save, snatching them out of the fire; and on some have mercy with fear."[143] As Christ's doing good to men's bodies ever aimed at winning their souls, all our ministry of love must be subordinated to that which is God's great purpose and longing—the salvation unto life eternal.

In this labour of love praying and working must ever go together. At times prayer may reach those whom the

141 "Let us consider": Hebrews 10:24.

142 "Even if a man...": Galatians 6:1.

143 "Some save...": Jude 1:23.

words cannot reach. At times prayer may chiefly be needed for ourselves, to obtain the wisdom and courage for the words. At times it may be specially called forth for the soul by the very lack of fruit from our words. As a rule, praying and working must be inseparable—the praying to obtain from God what we need for the soul; the working to bring to it what God has given us. The words of John here are most suggestive as to the power of prayer in our labour of love. It leads us to think of prayer as a personal work; with a very definite object; and a certainty of answer.

Let prayer be a personal effort. If any man see his brother he shall ask. We are so accustomed to act through societies and associations that we are in danger of losing sight of the duty resting upon each of us to watch over those around him. Every member of my body is ready to serve any other member. Every believer is to care for the fellow-believers who are within his reach, in his church, his house, or social circle. The sin of each is a loss and a hurt to the body of Christ. Let your eyes be open to the sins of your brethren around you; not to speak evil or judge or helplessly complain, but to love and help and care and pray. Ask God to see your brother's sin, in its sinfulness, its danger to himself, its grief to Christ, its loss to the body; but also as within reach of God's compassion and deliverance. Shutting our eyes to the sin of our brethren around us is not true love. See it, and take it to God, and make it part of your work for God to pray for your brother and seek new life for him.

Let prayer be definite. If any man see his brother sinning let him ask. We need prayer from a person for a person. Scripture and God's spirit teach us to pray for all society, for the Church with which we are associated, for nations, and for special spheres of work. Most needful and blessed. But somehow more is needed—to take of those with whom we come into contact, one by one, and make them the subjects of our intercession. The larger supplications[144] must have their place, but it is difficult with regard to them to know when our prayers are answered. But there is nothing will bring God so near, will test and strengthen our faith, and make us know we are fellow-workers with God, as when we receive an answer to our prayers for individuals. It will quicken in us the new and blessed consciousness that we indeed have power with God. Let every worker seek to exercise this grace of taking up and praying for individual souls. [1]

Count upon an answer. He shall ask, and God will give him (the one who prays) life for them that sin. The words follow on those in which John had spoken about the confidence we have of being heard, if we ask anything according to His will.[145] There is often complaint made of not knowing God's will. But here there is no difficulty. He willeth "that all men should be saved."[146] If we rest our faith on this will of God, we shall grow strong and grasp the promise. "He shall ask, and God will give him life for them that sin."[147] The Holy Spirit will lead us, if we yield ourselves to be led by Him, to the souls God would

144 **Supplications:** In this usage, prayers asking for something.

145 A reference to 1 John 5:14.

146 "that all men...": 1 Timothy 2:4.

147 "He shall ask...": 1 John 5:16.

---

1 This thought is very strikingly put in a penny tract, *One by One*, to be obtained from the author, Mr. Thomas Hogben, Welcome Mission, Portsmouth.
(Thomas Hogben was an evangelist who founded the One by One Working Band, a group devoted to personal evangelism.)

have us take as our special care, and for which the grace of faith and persevering prayer will be given us. Let the wonderful promise: God will give to him who asks life for them who sin, stir us and encourage us to our priestly ministry of personal and definite intercession, as one of the most blessed among the good works in which we can serve God and man.

Praying and working are inseparable. Let all who work learn to pray well. Let all who pray learn to work well.

1. To pray Thee confidently, and, if need be, perseveringly,[148] for an individual, needs a close walk with God, and the faith that we can prevail with Him.

2. In all our work for God, prayer must take a much larger place. If God is to work all; if our posture is to be that of entire dependence, waiting for Him to work in us; if it takes time to persevere and to receive in ourselves what God gives us for others; there needs to be a work and a labouring in prayer.

3. Oh that God would open our eyes to the glory of this work of saving souls, as the one thing God lives for, as the one thing He wants to work in us.

4. Let us pray for the love and power of God to come on us, for the blessed work of soul-winning.

148 **Perseveringly:** Repeatedly.

WORKING FOR GOD:
I KNOW THY WORKS

To the angel of the church in Ephesus—in
Thyatira—in Sardis—in Philadelphia—in
Laodicea write: I know thy works.[2]

REVELATION 2:3

"*I* know thy works." These are the words of Him who walketh in the midst of the seven golden candlesticks, and whose eyes are like a flame of fire. As He looks upon the churches, the first thing He sees and judges of is—the works. The works are the revelation of the life and character. If we are willing to bring our works into His holy presence, His words can teach us what our work ought to be.

To Ephesus He says: "I know thy works, and thy toil and patience, and that thou canst not bear evil men, and thou hast patience and didst bear for My name's

---

2   In the A. V. we find the words in all the seven epistles; according to R. V. they occur only five times.
    ("A.V.": The "authorized version" of the Bible—the King James Version that was for 300 years the main English translation used in the English-speaking world. "R.V.": An authorized revision of the King James version, created in England by some fifty Bible scholars and published between 1881 and 1885.)

sake, and hast not grown weary. But I have this against thee, that thou hast left thy first love. Repent, and do the first works."[149] There was here much to praise—toil, and patience, and zeal that had never grown weary. But there was one thing lacking—the tenderness of the first love.

149 "I know thy works [to the church at Ephesus]...": Revelation 2:2-5.

In His work for us Christ gave us before and above everything His love, the personal tender affection of His heart. In our work for Him He asks us nothing less. There is such a danger of work being carried on, and our even bearing much for Christ's sake, while the freshness of our love has passed away. And that is what Christ seeks. And that is what gives power. And that is what nothing can compensate for. Christ looks for the warm loving heart, the personal affection which ever keeps Him the centre of our love and joy.

Christian workers, see that all your work be the work of love, of tender personal devotion to Christ Jesus.

To Thyatira: "I know thy works, and thy love and faith and ministry and patience, and that the last works are more than the first. But I have this against thee, that thou sufferest the woman Jezebel, and she teacheth and seduceth My servants."[150] Here again the works are enumerated and praised: "the last had even been more than the first." But then there is one failure: a false toleration of what led to impurity and idolatry. And then He adds of His judgments: "the churches shall know that I am He which searches the reins and hearts; and I will give to each one of you according to your works."[151]

150 "I know thy works [to the church at Thyatira]...": Revelation 2:19, 20.

151 "the churches shall know...": Revelation 2:23.

Along with much of good works there may be some one form of error or evil tolerated which endangers the whole church. In Ephesus there was zeal for orthodoxy, but a lack of love; here love and faith, but a lack of faithfulness against error. If good works are to please our Lord, if our whole life must be in harmony with them, in entire separation from the world and its allurements,[152] we must seek to be what He promised to make us, stablished in every good word and work. Our work will decide our estimate in His judgment.

To Sardis: "I know thy works, that thou hast a name to live, and thou art dead. Be watchful and stablish the things that are ready to die: for I have found no works of thine fulfilled before My God."[153]

There may be all the forms of godliness without the power; all the activities of religious organisation without the life. There may be many works, and yet He may say: I have found no work of thine fulfilled before My God, none that can stand the test and be really acceptable to God as a spiritual sacrifice. In Ephesus it was works lacking in love, in Thyatira works lacking in purity, in Sardis works lacking in life.

To Philadelphia: "I know thy works, that thou hast a little power, and didst keep My word and didst not deny My name. Because thou didst keep My word, I also will keep thee."[154]

On earth Jesus had said: "He that hath My commandments and keepeth them, he it is that loveth Me. If a man love Me, he will keep My word. and My Father will love him."[155] Philadelphia, the church for which there is no reproof, had this mark: its chief work, and the law of all its work, was, it kept Christ's word, not in an orthodox

152   **Allurements:** Enticing fascinations.

153   "I know thy works [to the church at Sardis]...": Revelation 3:1-2.

154   "I know thy works [to the church at Philadelphia]...": Revelation 3:8, 10.

155   "He that hath My commandments...": John 14:21.

creed only, but in practical obedience. Let nothing less, let this truly, be the mark and spirit of all our work: a keeping of the word of Christ. Full, loving conformity to His will will be rewarded.

To Laodicea: "I know thy works, that thou art neither cold nor hot. Thou sayest, I am rich and have gotten riches, and have need of nothing."[156] There is not a church without its works, its religious activities.

And yet the two great marks of Laodicean religion, lukewarmness, and its natural accompaniment, self-complacence, may rob them of their worth. It not only, like Ephesus, teaches us the need of a fresh and fervent love, but also the need of that poverty of spirit, that conscious weakness out of which the absolute dependence on Christ's strength for all our work will grow, and which will no longer leave Christ standing at the door, but enthrone Him in the Heart.

"I know thy works." He who tested the works of the seven churches still lives and watches over us. He is ready in His love to discover what is lacking, to give timely warning and help, and to teach us the path in which our works can be fulfilled before His God. Let us learn from Ephesus the lesson of fervent love to Christ, from Thyatira that of purity and separation from all evil, from Sardis that of the need of true life to give worth to work, from Philadelphia that of keeping His word, and from Laodicea that of the poverty of spirit which possesses the kingdom of heaven, and gives Christ the throne of all! Workers! Let us live and work in Christ's presence. He will teach and correct and help us, and one day give the full reward of all our works because they were His own works in us.

156 "I know thy works [to the church at Laodicea]..." Revelation 3:15, 17.

WORKING FOR GOD: THAT GOD MAY BE GLORIFIED

If any man serveth, let him serve as of the strength which God supplieth: that in all things God may be glorified through Jesus Christ, whose is the glory and dominion for ever and ever. Amen.

1 PETER 4:11

*W*ORK is not done for its own sake. Its value consists in the object it attains. The purpose of him who commands or performs the work gives it its real worth. And the clearer a man's insight into the purpose, the better fitted will he be to take charge of the higher parts of the work. In the erection of some splendid building, the purpose of the day-labourer[157] may simply be as a hireling to earn his wages. The trained stone-cutter has a higher object: be thinks of the beauty and perfection of the work he does. The master mason has a wider range of thought: his aim is that all the masonry shall be true and good. The contractor for the whole building has a higher aim—that the whole building shall perfectly correspond to the plan he has to carry out. The architect has had a

157 **Day-labourer:** People employed on a temporary, day-by-day basis; often unskilled labor.

still higher purpose—that the great principles of art and beauty might find their full expression in material shape. With the owner we find the final end—the use to which the grand structure is to be put when he, say, presents the building as a gift for the benefit of his townsmen. All who have worked upon the building honestly have done so with some true purpose. The deeper the insight and the keener the interest in the ultimate design, the more important the share in the work, and the greater the joy in carrying it out.

Peter tells us what our aim ought to be in all Christian service—"that in all things God may be glorified through Jesus Christ." In the work of God, a work not to be done for wages but for love, the humblest labourer is admitted to a share in God's plans, and to an insight into the great purpose which God is working out. That purpose is nothing less than this: that God may be glorified. This is the one purpose of God, the great worker in heaven, the source and master of all work, that the glory of His love and power and blessing may be shown. This is the one purpose of Christ, the great worker on earth in human nature, the example and leader of all our work. This is the great purpose of the Holy Spirit, the power that worketh in us, or, as Peter says here, "the strength that God supplieth." As this becomes our deliberate, intelligent purpose, our work will rise to its true level, and lift us into living fellowship with God.

"That in all things God may be glorified." What does this mean? The glory of God is this, that He alone is the Living One, who has life in Himself. Yet not for Himself alone, but, because His life is love, for the creatures as much as for Himself. This is the glory of God, that He is the alone and ever-flowing fountain of all life and goodness and happiness, and that His creatures can have all this only as He gives it and works it in them. His working all in all, this is His glory. And the only glory His creature, His child, can give Him is this—receiving all He is willing to give, yielding to Him to let Him work, and then acknowledging that He has done it. Thus God Himself shows forth His glory in us; in our willing surrender to Him, and our joyful acknowledgment that He does all, we glorify Him. And so our life and work is glorified, as it has one purpose with all God's own work, that in all things God may be glorified, "whose is the glory for ever and ever."

See here now the spirit that ennobles and consecrates Christian service according to Peter: "He that serveth (in ministering to the saints or the needy), let him serve as of the strength which God supplieth." Let me cultivate a deep conviction that God's work, down into the details of daily life, can only be done in God's strength, by the power of the Spirit working in us. Let me believe firmly and unceasingly that the Holy Spirit does dwell in me, as the power from on high, for all work to be done for on high. Let me in my Christian work fear nothing so much, as working in my own human will and strength, and so losing the one thing needful in my work, God working in me. Let me rejoice in the weakness that renders me so absolutely dependent upon such a God, and wait in prayer for His power to take full possession.

"Let him serve as of the strength which God supplieth, that in all things God may be glorified through Jesus Christ." The more you depend on God alone for your strength, the more will He be glorified. The more you seek to make God's purpose your purpose, the more will you be led to give way to His working and His strength and love. Oh! that every, the feeblest, worker might see what a nobility it gives to work, what a new glory to life, what a new urgency and joy in labouring for souls, when the one purpose has mastered us: that in all things God may be glorified through Jesus Christ.

1. The glory of God as Creator was seen in His making man in His own image. The glory of God as Redeemer is seen in the work He carries on for saving men, and bringing them to Himself.

2. This glory is the glory of His holy love, casting sin out of the heart, and dwelling there.

3. The only glory we can bring to God is to yield ourselves to His redeeming love to take possession of us, to fill us with love to others, and so through us to show forth His glory.

4. Let this be the one end of our lives—to glorify God; in living to work for Him, "as of the strength which God supplieth"; and winning souls to know and live for His glory.

5. Lord! teach us to serve in the strength which God supplieth, that God in all things may be glorified through Jesus Christ, whose is the glory for ever and ever. Amen.

READING PLAN AND DISCUSSION QUESTIONS

*I*n your small group or book club, consider using the following reading plan along with the suggested questions to help prime the pump and get the conversation started.

Waiting on God

Session One (Days 1-5)

• What leapt off the page for you in these chapters?

• What—if anything—did you find challenging?

• Murray suggests that there is no good but that good which God works. Do you agree… or not? Why do you answer as you do?

• The author writes, "There may be much praying with but very little waiting on God." How well would you say that describes your relationship with God?

Session Two (Days 6-10)

• What leapt off the page for you in these chapters?

• What—if anything—did you find challenging?

• Murray writes, "We are so accustomed to judge of God and His work in us by what we feel, that the great probability is that when we begin more to cultivate the waiting on Him, we shall be discouraged." Has that been your experience as you've focused on waiting on God? If so, what do you think might help your discouragement?

• Murray suggests there's a difference between the "religion of the mind" and the "religion of the heart." How would you define each? Which do you find most comfortable...and most challenging? Why?

Session Three (Days 11-15)

• What leapt off the page for you in these chapters?

• What—if anything—did you find challenging?

• Murray warns that we can limit God when we confine our desires and prayers to our own thoughts of them. Do you agree with Murray? Give an example of why you answer as you do.

• Murray suggests we wait on God for His counsel. How do you access God's counsel? What's counsel you've received that directly addressed a concern you were experiencing?

Session Four (Days 16-21)

• What leapt off the page for you in these chapters?

• What—if anything—did you find challenging?

• Murray writes about waiting for God when experiencing dark times. Describe a time God met you during a difficult time—or hasn't that happened for you?

• Murray writes this: "GOD is a God of mercy and a God of judgment." How have you primarily experienced God: as a God of mercy or a God of judgement?

Session Five (Days 22-26)

• What leapt off the page for you in these chapters?

• What—if anything—did you find challenging?

• Murray suggests that God is prepared to give more than we can imagine or anticipate. In what ways, if any, has God blessed you beyond your expectations or imaginings?

• Waiting on God quietly...how well do you do that? Would the people who know you best say you're apt to patiently wait for something to happen? Would God say so?

Session Six (Days 27-31)

• What leapt off the page for you in these chapters?

• What—if anything—did you find challenging?

• Murray writes: It is always easier to be engaged with the religion of the past or the future than to be faithful in the religion of today. What's your reaction to that statement?

• Murray warns of two great enemies: the World and Self. Of those two adversaries, which do you find most effective at interfering with your ability to wait on God?

Working for God

Session One (Days 1-5)

• What leapt off the page for you in these chapters?

• What—if anything—did you find challenging?

• The author writes, "God's work can only be done in God's strength, by God Himself working in us." Do you agree? If so, what implications does that have in whatever work you're doing in the church—or outside the church—to advance the Kingdom?

• Murry reminds us that we work to the extent of our abilities. What abilities do you have that can be used to work for God? How are you employing them?

Session Two (Days 6-10)

• What leapt off the page for you in these chapters?

• What—if anything—did you find challenging?

• Murray writes, "Doing is the best teacher. If you want to know how to do a thing, begin and do it." Do you think that's good advice? How has it worked out in your life?

• Murray reminds us of the Biblical truth that we're created for good works. In your own life, what do you think those works might be? What are you drawn to do given your unique blend of talents, skills, and gifts?

Session Three (Days 11-15)

• What leapt off the page for you in these chapters?

• What—if anything—did you find challenging?

• Murray asserts that "no works can have any worth but as they come of love." Do you agree? Why or why not?

• Murray writes, "Humility makes us willing to serve; love makes us wise to know how to do it." Tell about a time you were humbled…and a time love guided you to serve in a way that made a difference.

Session Four (Days 16-21)

• What leapt off the page for you in these chapters?

• What—if anything—did you find challenging?

• The author writes, "The gospel never takes away anything from us without giving us something better in its stead." Has that been your experience as you follow Christ? Give an example of how this statement has been true—or untrue—in your life.

• Murray wrote this more than a hundred years ago: "There are thousands of Christians to-day who feel that their own business is urgent, and must be attended to, and have no conception of the urgency of Christ's work committed to them." How relevant do you think those words are today? Why? How relevant are they to you personally?

Session Five (Days 22-26)
• What leapt off the page for you in these chapters?

• What—if anything—did you find challenging?

• On Day 23, Murray gives four specific pieces of advice for working for God. Which strikes you as most relevant to your current situation? Why?

• Murray reminds us that God works well through our weaknesses when we rely on Him. How have you seen that play out in your life?

Session Six (Days 27-31)

• What leapt off the page for you in these chapters?

• What—if anything—did you find challenging?

• Murray writes, "GOD created us not to contemplate but to act." Do you agree? Disagree? What are your thoughts?

•. Respond to this observation by the author: "We are so accustomed to act through societies and associations that we are in danger of losing sight of the duty resting upon each of us to watch over those around him."